Write-In Reader

Grade 4

Printed in the U.S.A.

ISBN 978-0-547-87422-7

13 0928 21 20 19 18 17 16 15

4500522599   A B C D E F G

HOUGHTON MIFFLIN HARCOURT
School Publishers

Be a Reading Detective!

Welcome to your *Write-In Reader*! With this book, you will be a **Reading Detective**. You will look for clues in stories and in nonfiction selections. The clues will help you

- ▷ **enjoy stories,**

- ▷ **understand nonfiction,**

- ▷ **answer questions, and**

- ▷ **be a great reader!**

A Reading Detective can solve the mystery of any reading selection. No selection is too hard! A Reading Detective **asks questions**. A Reading Detective **reads carefully**.

Asking questions and reading carefully will help you **find clues**. Then, you will

- ▷ **stop,**

- ▷ **think, and**

- ▷ **write!**

Let's try it! Follow the trail . . .

In the box is the beginning of a story. Read carefully. Ask yourself questions:

▷ **Who is the story about?**

▷ **Where and when does the story take place?**

▷ **What is happening?**

Look for clues to answer your questions.

> Logan was enjoying his bike ride. He felt the warm sun on his face. He smelled the beach nearby. He heard his dad humming on the bike in front of him. So far, Logan was having a great birthday.
>
> Suddenly, Logan screeched to a stop.
>
> "Dad!" he called out. "Look at that!"

Stop Think Write

Where and when does the story take place? How do you know?

_____

_____

Did you read carefully? Did you look for clues? Did the clues help you answer the questions? If they did, you are already a **Reading Detective**!

Contents

✓ **TARGET VOCABULARY**

**mention
mood
peculiar
positive
talent**

Child Actors

1 A child can become an actor from the time he or she is a baby. Any baby can play a baby. A baby does not need acting **talent** to cry or sleep!

What special talent do you have?

_____

_____

_____

2 A baby cannot be in the bright lights too long. That is why most babies in movies or TV shows are played by identical twins or triplets. They take turns being in the spotlight. If one baby gets in a bad **mood** on the set, the mother can trade him or her with a sibling!

What puts you in a good mood?

_____

_____

_____

3 A **peculiar** fact about child actors is that they have teachers come to them right on the set! When they are busy acting, there is no time to go to school.

What is a peculiar animal you know?

_____

4 You might think it is great to miss school. However, child actors are **positive** that it is no fun. They do not get to make many friends. They also miss out on joining clubs.

What activity do you feel positive that you will do this year?

_____

_____

5 Some child actors get to travel around the world to film movies. In interviews, adult and child actors **mention** that this is one of their favorite parts of the job.

What is another word for mention?

_____

Paige Starts Over

by Carol Alexander

Paige stepped out of her father's car. The low brick building looked welcoming. The fields around the school were grassy and green.

Paige thought, "It looks just the way a school should."

Her father called out, "Should I come in with you?"

"No, I'll be fine," Paige replied.

Outside the classroom door, Paige took a deep breath. "Act like you've done this before," she told herself.

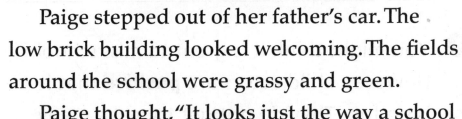

Stop Think Write

STORY STRUCTURE

Where does the story take place? How do you know?

_____

_____

_____

4

Brightly colored art hung on the walls. The room was sunny and warm. It matched Paige's happy **mood**.

"Please come in," said the teacher. "Class, this is—"

"That's Paige Bridges!" someone shouted.

Uh oh! Paige had been hoping to blend in. That was going to be tough. She had been a child star on television, playing the part of a little girl named Sophie. The show had become one of TV's most popular comedies.

Stop | **Think** | **Write**

VOCABULARY

In what way does the classroom match Paige's <u>mood</u>?

_____

_____

_____

Paige felt everyone stare at her. This was all so new. When you're an actor, there is no time for school. In Hollywood, a tutor had come to her home. Going to school was different.

Paige sat down in an empty seat, her face growing red.

All day, kids came up to her, excited to meet a star. "Tell that joke Sophie used to tell! Make a Sophie face!" the kids begged. They all loved Sophie. Did they even like Paige?

Stop | Think | Write

STORY STRUCTURE

What problem does Paige face?

_____

_____

_____

They had math that afternoon. The girl next to her pushed her book over. "I'm Maria," she whispered. "I loved your show, Paige. Do you like math?"

Paige said, "That's my favorite subject."

"Mine, too!" Maria answered. "We can do this problem together. Look, if we round up this number—"

"We get 3,000!" Paige said. "I'm **positive** that's right."

Maria grinned and nodded.

Stop | **Think** | **Write**

VOCABULARY

Why is Paige positive she has found the correct answer?

_____

_____

_____

Maria and Paige left the building together at three o'clock. Two girls called out, "There's Sophie! Hey, Sophie!" Paige's smile faded.

"Listen, Paige," Maria said. "Do you like to swim?"

"I love swimming! That's my number one **talent**!"

"Well, why not join the swim team? It's really fun."

Paige enjoyed being on the team. At first, however, the other swimmers only wanted to talk about Sophie.

Stop **Think** **Write**

STORY STRUCTURE

How does life begin to change for Paige?

_____

_____

_____

Maria helped. Whenever anyone started to **mention** Sophie, Maria shook her head. "Talk to Paige. She's a real person!"

It was the first time Paige had had a best friend.

Soon, the others forgot she was a star. Paige forgot about that, too. She was busy with swim meets, art class, and the science fair. She and a girl named Trina won a prize for their project about frogs. Paige felt proud.

Stop | Think | Write

STORY STRUCTURE

Why does Paige forget about being a star?

_____

_____

_____

One day, a boy moved next door. He came over to talk to Paige. "Hi, I'm Christopher." Then a **peculiar** thing happened. He asked, "What's your name?"

Paige's mouth dropped open. How amazing! "Where are you from?" she asked.

"My parents are news reporters. We've lived in countries all over the world," the boy said. "This is my first time in the United States."

"Well, I'm Paige," she said simply.

"I'm glad to meet you, Paige."

"Welcome to Maple Hills," said Paige.

Stop **Think** **Write**

UNDERSTANDING CHARACTERS

Why is Paige amazed when Christopher asks her name?

_____

_____

_____

Look Back and Respond

1 What changes for Paige when she moves to Maple Hills from Hollywood?

Hint
For clues, see pages 5 and 6.

_____

_____

_____

2 How does Paige want to be treated?

Hint
Clues are on almost every page! See, for example, pages 4, 5, 9, and 10.

_____

_____

_____

3 How does Maria's friendship help Paige get used to her new life?

Hint
For clues, see pages 8 and 9.

_____

_____

_____

4 Do you know anyone like Paige? Explain.

Hint
Think about someone you know who had a hard time fitting in.

_____

_____

_____

Be a Reading Detective!

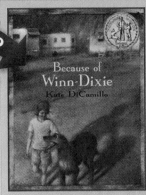
Return to

"Because of Winn-Dixie"
Student Book pp. 21–31

1 **What does Winn-Dixie do at the beginning of the story?**

☐ He looks in the library window.

☐ He nuzzles Miss Franny Block's feet.

☐ He chases a bear away from the library.

Prove It! What evidence in the story supports your answer?
Check the boxes. ✓   Make notes.

Evidence	Notes
☐ the library's rule about dogs	
☐ what Miss Franny does and says	
☐ what the narrator tells us	
☐	

Write About It!

STORY STRUCTURE

Answer question **1** using evidence from the text.

_____

_____

_____

_____

_____

_____

2 **Which event happens first?**

☐ Opal and Miss Franny decide to be friends.

☐ Miss Franny tells Opal the story about the bear.

☐ Miss Franny is frightened by Winn-Dixie.

☐ Miss Franny is frightened by a bear.

Prove It! What evidence in the story supports your answer? Check the boxes. ☑ Make notes.

Evidence	Notes
☐ Miss Franny Block's words	
☐ events in the story	
☐ words like "a long time ago"	
☐	

Write About It!

SEQUENCE OF EVENTS

Answer question **2** using evidence from the text.

_____

_____

_____

_____

_____

_____

_____

dream
example
injustice
numerous
preferred

The Black Arts Movement

1 The Black Arts Movement began in the 1960s. Black artists saw **injustice**. They saw African Americans being treated badly. They wanted to help.

Write a word that means the opposite of injustice.

_____

2 These artists were proud to be African American. They wanted to set an **example**. Their work was about African American life.

Tell about a time when you set an example for someone.

_____

_____

_____

3 It was the first time so many African American artists joined in a common cause. They **preferred** to show their pride in their culture through their work.

Tell about a food that you <u>preferred</u>.

_____

_____

_____

4 The movement had **numerous** artists. There were poets, actors, musicians, and dancers. They all had a similar message.

Have you belonged to a group with <u>numerous</u> people? Explain.

_____

_____

_____

5 These artists had a **dream**. They wanted their community to be proud and strong.

What is your <u>dream</u>?

_____

_____

_____

Gwendolyn Brooks

by Mia Lewis

A Prize-Winning Poet

Gwendolyn Brooks was a poet. She wrote many books of poetry. In 1950, she won a big award for a book called *Annie Allen*. It was the Pulitzer Prize. She was the first black poet to win this prize.

Winning the Pulitzer changed her life. She joked about it. "Sometimes I feel my name is Gwendolyn Pulitzer Brooks," she said.

Stop | **Think** | **Write**

AUTHOR'S PURPOSE

Why does the author include Gwendolyn Brooks's own words about getting the Pulitzer Prize?

_____

_____

_____

Early Poems

Brooks was born in 1917. She grew up in Chicago. She started making up rhymes at an early age. Her mother and father helped her. They taught her to read and write.

Her first poem was printed in a Chicago newspaper when she was 13. By the time she was 17, she had published 75 poems.

Brooks was brave. She sent her work to Langston Hughes, a famous poet. He told her to keep writing!

Stop **Think** **Write**

CONCLUSIONS AND GENERALIZATIONS

How do you think Gwendolyn Brooks felt when she sent her work to Langston Hughes?

_____

_____

_____

Bronzeville

Gwendolyn Brooks went to college. Later she married and had two children. She also followed Hughes's advice. She kept on writing! Her first book came out in 1945. A book of poems for children came out a few years later.

Both books were about Bronzeville, an African American neighborhood in Chicago. The poems brought the town to life. They told about the people.

Stop **Think** **Write**

Why do you think the author includes information about Bronzeville?

_____

_____

_____

Poetic Voice

Brooks felt poetry should be read out loud. She loved to read her poems to people. She read wherever people would listen. She read in schools. She read in hospitals. She read in apartment buildings.

She took her poems wherever she went. She was always ready to read!

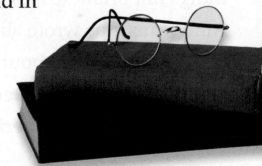

Stop **Think** **Write**

CAUSE AND EFFECT

Why did Gwendolyn Brooks take her poems wherever she went?

_____

_____

_____

The Black Arts Movement

Gwendolyn Brooks went to a meeting in 1967. She met many young poets there. These poets were very proud to be black. They wrote about things that were important to black Americans.

These poets were part of the Black Arts Movement. They set an **example** for Brooks. She had always written about African American life. Now she began to write more about things important to African Americans. She wrote about the way they were treated. She wrote about **injustice**. She did not want people to be treated unfairly just because they were African American.

Stop | Think | Write

How did the poets of the Black Arts Movement set an **example** for Brooks?

_____

_____

_____

Spreading the Word

Brooks became important in the Black Arts Movement. She **preferred** to have her books printed by African American printers. She worked with young African American poets. She said she learned a lot from young people.

Brooks ran poetry workshops and held poetry contests. Mostly she held the contests in schools. Once she held a contest in a prison. She often paid for the prizes with her own money.

Stop   Think   Write

AUTHOR'S PURPOSE

Do you think the author feels that the Black Arts Movement was important? Explain.

_____

_____

_____

An Inspiration to Others

Brooks kept writing books for children. She told children to be proud of who they were. She gave advice to young poets. She said, "Talk about what you wonder."

Brooks won **numerous** awards. She was given many honors. She even had a school named after her! It was her **dream** to help others. Her dream came true. She helped many writers. She inspired black poets to write about their own lives.

Stop **Think** **Write**

How did Gwendolyn Brooks's <u>dream</u> come true?

_____

_____

_____

_____

Look Back and Respond

1 **What was Bronzeville?**

Hint

For clues, look on page 16.

_____

_____

_____

2 **Why did Brooks read poetry in many places?**

Hint

For a clue, see page 17.

_____

_____

_____

3 **Why was Gwendolyn Brooks an inspiration to young black writers?**

Hint

What did Brooks write about? How might her success have affected others?

_____

_____

_____

4 **What does the author think about Gwendolyn Brooks? How can you tell?**

Hint

You can find clues on every page!

_____

_____

_____

Be a Reading Detective!

Return to

"My Brother Martin"
Student Book pp. 49–61

1 **What is the author's main purpose on pages 54–57?**

- ☐ to give a history of racism in the South
- ☐ to show an event that changed King's life
- ☐ to describe King's childhood neighborhood

Prove It! What evidence in the selection supports your answer? Check the boxes. ✓ Make notes.

Evidence	Notes
☐ events in the neighborhood	
☐ what M.L. says and does	
☐ what Mother Dear says	
☐	

Write About It!

AUTHOR'S PURPOSE

Answer question **1** using evidence from the text.

_____

_____

_____

_____

_____

_____

_____

2 The author says that when she was young, there were laws that kept black people separate from white people. Is this a fact or an opinion?

☐ fact

☐ opinion

Prove It! What evidence in the selection supports your
answer? Check the boxes. ☑ Make notes.

Evidence	Notes
☐ details about theaters and parks	
☐ details about the neighborhood	
☐ what Mother Dear says	
☐ Daddy's dinnertime stories	
☐	

Write About It!

FACT AND OPINION

Answer question **2** using evidence from the text.

_____

_____

_____

_____

_____

_____

21B

Lesson 3

✓ **TARGET VOCABULARY**

access
isolated
obtain
remote
virtual

Children Who Need Books

In some communities around the world, it is often difficult for children to get, or **①** _____, books or other educational materials. Even online **②** _____ classrooms are not always possible. These regions are so far away, or **③** _____, that they do not have **④** _____ to electricity. People who live in these places can feel cut off and **⑤** _____ from each other and from the world around them.

6 May I have _____ to the computer room this afternoon?

7 Without her computer, she felt totally _____ from the world.

8 You must _____ your parents' permission in order to go on the class trip.

9 The area was so _____ that it did not even have electricity.

10 The _____ classroom is a great way for students who live in rural areas to stay connected.

Spreading the Words

by Dina McClellan

When she was 12 years old, a California student named Tatiana Grossman learned something that shocked her. She learned that 75 percent of children in some African countries could not read or write. This was because they lived in areas so **remote** that they lacked **access** to books.

Tatiana also learned that poor reading was a big problem in many countries, especially in parts of Africa. For instance, in **isolated** areas of Botswana and Lesotho, about two out of every five people could not read or write.

Stop **Think** **Write**

VOCABULARY

Which two highlighted words on this page mean the same thing? What do they mean?

_____

_____

_____

24

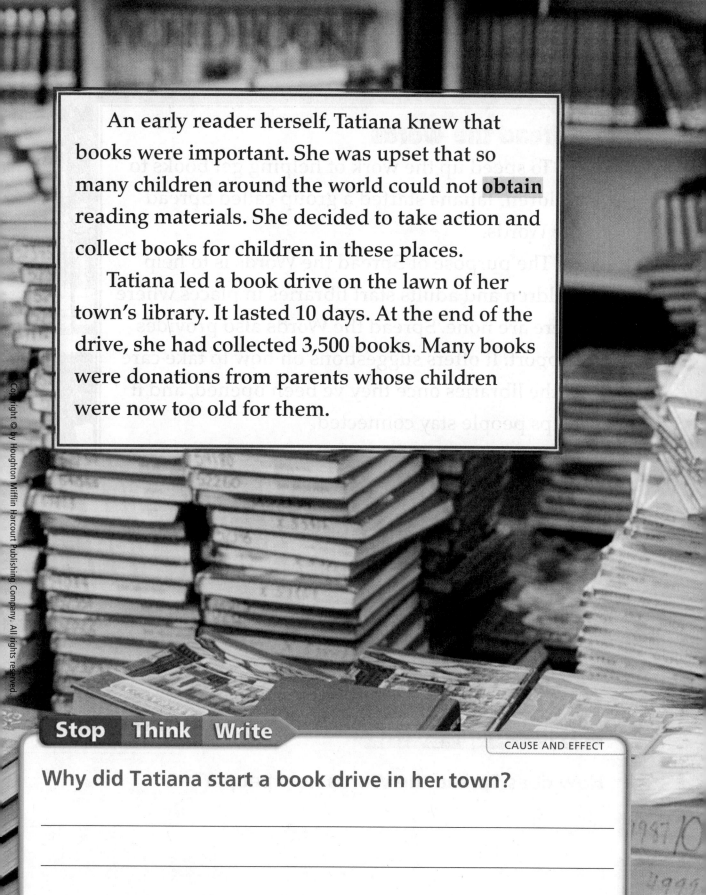

An early reader herself, Tatiana knew that books were important. She was upset that so many children around the world could not **obtain** reading materials. She decided to take action and collect books for children in these places.

Tatiana led a book drive on the lawn of her town's library. It lasted 10 days. At the end of the drive, she had collected 3,500 books. Many books were donations from parents whose children were now too old for them.

Stop **Think** **Write**

CAUSE AND EFFECT

Why did Tatiana start a book drive in her town?

_____

_____

_____

Spread the Words

To speed up the work of helping get books to children, Tatiana started a group called Spread the Words.

The purpose of Spread the Words is to help children and adults start libraries in places where there are none. Spread the Words also provides support. It offers suggestions on how to take care of the libraries once they've been opened, and it helps people stay connected.

Stop | **Think** | **Write**

MAIN IDEAS AND DETAILS

How does Spread the Words help people?

_____

_____

_____

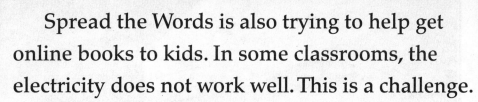

Spread the Words is also trying to help get online books to kids. In some classrooms, the electricity does not work well. This is a challenge.

Solving this challenge will get much-needed online books to those classrooms quickly. It will also avoid the high costs of shipping heavy books overseas.

Stop | Think | Write

Why is it sometimes hard to use online books in classrooms?

_____

_____

_____

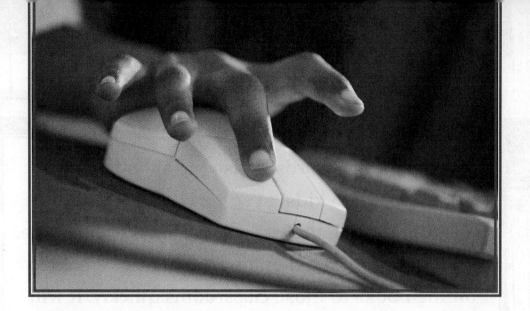

Going Digital

Today, as a teenager, Tatiana is busy working with school teachers and others. They are trying to provide classrooms with **virtual** teaching materials.

To further these goals, Tatiana is developing a small, easy-to-use, battery-operated electronic device. This device is loaded with textbooks, videos, and picture books. The Botswana Ministry of Education will test the technology.

Stop | **Think** | **Write**

CAUSE AND EFFECT

What effect might the new technology have?

_____

_____

_____

Spread the Words has opened libraries in five African countries. These libraries serve 115 schools and villages.

Tatiana has won many awards, including the World of Children Award (2011) and the Youth Assembly at the United Nations Award (2011). In 2010 she was a finalist for the International Children's Peace Prize. She has spoken with thousands of children and adults in the United States and Africa.

Stop | Think | Write

CONCLUSIONS AND GENERALIZATIONS

What can you conclude about Tatiana from reading this article?

_____

_____

_____

_____

29

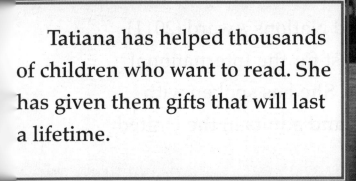

Tatiana has helped thousands of children who want to read. She has given them gifts that will last a lifetime.

Stop Think Write

INFER AND PREDICT

What does the author mean by "gifts that will last a lifetime"?

_____

_____

_____

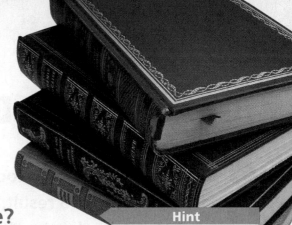

Look Back and Respond

1 **Why did Tatiana lead a book drive?**

Hint

For clues, look on page 24.

_____

_____

_____

2 **What is the purpose of Spread the Words?**

Hint

For clues, see pages 26 and 27.

_____

_____

_____

3 **Why do you think the author mentions the awards Tatiana has won?**

Hint

To help you answer the question, reread page 29.

_____

_____

_____

My Librarian Is a Camel
How Books Are Brought to Children Around the World
by Margriet Ruurs

Be a Reading Detective!

1 **Some communities are too small and isolated to have a library. As a result, they have different ways of getting books. What are these ways?**

"My Librarian Is a Camel"
Student Book pp. 79–91

☐ by mail   ☐ by camel

☐ by elephant   ☐ _____

Prove It! What evidence in the selection supports your answer? Check the boxes. ☑ Make notes.

Evidence	Notes
☐ details about Canada	
☐ details about Thailand	
☐ details about Kenya	
☐	

Write About It!

CAUSE AND EFFECT

Answer question 1 using evidence from the text.

_____

_____

_____

_____

_____

_____

_____

2 What can you learn about each country from the graphic features in the selection?

☐ the shape of the country

☐ details about how children get books

☐ what the flag looks like

☐ other _____

Prove It! What evidence in the selection supports your answer? Check the boxes. ☑ Make notes.

Evidence	Notes
☐ photographs	
☐ maps	
☐ illustrations	
☐	

Write About It!

TEXT AND GRAPHIC FEATURES

Answer question **2** using evidence from the text.

_____

_____

_____

_____

_____

_____

✓ TARGET VOCABULARY

assist
favor
misjudged
prior
scheme

Food Banks

Prior to starting a food bank, John van Hengel helped out in a soup kitchen. He discovered that grocery stores throw away edible food. He asked them to donate that food to the soup kitchen.

The soup kitchen was soon overloaded with food! John **misjudged** the amount of food he needed. He ended up with far more food than he could use.

John began to think up a **scheme**. What if he could store food in the same way that a bank stores money? Then the food would be there for hungry people when they needed it.

He also asked farmers to do him a **favor**. He asked for their extra food. With this food, he started St. Mary's Food Bank, the country's first food bank.

St. Mary's got money from a grant. This money was used to **assist** in starting 18 new food banks. Today the Phoenix food bank alone hands out over 70 million pounds of food each year!

1 John thought of a _____ to store food for hungry people.

2 John worked in a soup kitchen _____ to starting a food bank.

3 John _____ how much food he would need and ended up with too much.

4 What is the last <u>favor</u> you did for a friend?

_____

_____

_____

5 How might you <u>assist</u> a student who is new to your school?

_____

_____

_____

Concert for a Cause

by Estelle Kleinman

Narrator: We're in Ben's kitchen. He and Amy are talking about a school project.

Amy: I'm glad we're finished with this report. I never knew that so many people in the world go hungry every day. It's so sad!

Ben: There are hungry people right where we live!

Amy: I wish we could do something to help.

Narrator: Ben gets excited as a **scheme** begins to take shape in his mind.

Ben: I think we can!

Characters

Narrator
Ben, a fourth grader
Amy, Ben's friend
Grandpa

Stop | **Think** | **Write**

VOCABULARY

What do you think Ben's <u>scheme</u> is about?

_____

_____

_____

34

Ben: Amy, I play the trumpet and sing. You have a great voice, too. Do me a **favor** and make a list of people you know who can play an instrument.

Amy: Slow down, Ben! What's this all about?

Ben: We can put on a concert to raise money for the local food bank!

Amy: What a great idea! I'm sure your grandpa will help, too. Didn't he once play in a band?

Narrator: Ben's grandpa was thrilled with the idea. Amy and Ben got others to join in, too.

Stop | Think | Write

UNDERSTANDING CHARACTERS

How are Ben and Amy alike?

_____

_____

_____

Narrator: The musicians need a lot of practice.

At rehearsal, Ben is more than a little on edge.

Ben: No, no. Someone is off key. We have to start over.

Amy: Take it easy, Ben. We're all trying our best.

Ben: Your best isn't good enough! Maybe I **misjudged** your talent.

Narrator: Amy storms out.

Grandpa: Ben, that wasn't nice.

Ben: I know, Grandpa. I just want things to go well.

Let's keep practicing. I'll apologize to Amy later.

Stop **Think** **Write**

Why does Amy storm out?

_____

_____

_____

Narrator: It is now a week **prior** to the concert. Ben has still not spoken to Amy. He and his grandpa are practicing.

Grandpa: You should call Amy.

Ben: I don't know, Grandpa. I think I'll do that after the concert.

Narrator: Grandpa shakes his head.

Grandpa: You shouldn't put important things off. You are being thoughtful to have a concert to help others. But you shouldn't forget about Amy. She's your friend.

Narrator: Just then, Grandpa gets dizzy and falls to the floor.

Ben: Grandpa! Are you okay? I'll go get help!

Stop **Think** **Write**

THEME

What point is Grandpa trying to make to Ben?

_____

_____

_____

Narrator: Ben's grandpa goes to the hospital. When the day of the concert arrives, Ben is surprised to see Amy at the auditorium.

Amy: I just heard about your grandpa. How is he?

Ben: He'll be fine. However, he has to miss the concert.

Amy: I know I can't take his place, but I'd like to **assist** you if I can. I know this is a big deal.

Ben: Well, we sure are missing a great female voice. Do you remember the songs we were practicing?

Amy: Sure do! I'll get ready.

Narrator: Ben wants to say more to Amy, but the concert is about to begin.

Stop | Think | Write

In what different ways might Amy <u>assist</u> Ben?

_____

_____

_____

Narrator: About 100 people come to the concert. It is a big success. Ben and Amy talk backstage.

Ben: You were great! The concert wouldn't have been as good without you. Thanks for helping out.

Amy: That's what friends do—help each other.

Ben: Well, I wasn't a very good friend. I'm sorry.

Amy: I can't argue with that. Still, I forgive you. How much did we make for the food bank?

Ben: We raised $700! That's enough to buy 2,800 pounds of food!

Amy: Wow! Let's go see your grandpa and tell him the good news.

Stop | Think | Write

THEME

What lesson has Ben learned?

_____

_____

_____

Hunger Facts

- About 37 million people in the U.S. go hungry. That means they miss meals, eat less than they want, or even go entire days without food.
- Of the people who go hungry, 12 million are children.

Feeding America

Feeding America is the largest group to give food to the hungry. It gives food to more than 25 million people a year.

Who Helps Food Banks?

- The food industry provides extra or unwanted grocery items.
- Companies give money to buy food.
- People give money, food, or time to help out.

Stop Think Write

THEME

How do these facts help you understand why Ben put on the concert?

_____

_____

_____

Look Back and Respond

1 How would you describe Ben?

_____

_____

_____

Hint

Clues you can use are on almost every page! See, for example, pages 34, 36, and 39.

2 Do you think that Amy and Ben have a good friendship? Explain.

_____

_____

_____

Hint

You can find clues on pages 35, 38, and 39.

3 What does the play say about friendship?

_____

_____

_____

Hint

Your answer to question 2 should help you.

4 What kinds of things could you do to help out where you live?

_____

_____

_____

Hint

Think about what you could do to make your community better.

Be a Reading Detective!

Return to

"The Power of W.O.W.!"
Student Book pp. 111–121

1 What important message about life can you learn from the play?

☐ One person can make a difference.

☐ A car wash can raise money.

☐ For successful fundraising, get publicity.

Prove It! What evidence in the play supports your answer?
Check the boxes. ☑ Make notes.

Evidence	Notes
☐ what Ileana cares about	
☐ what Ileana says and does	
☐ how the play ends	
☐	

Write About It!

THEME

Answer question **1** using evidence from the text.

_____

_____

_____

_____

_____

_____

_____

2 **What can you conclude about Mrs. Nguyen?**

☐ She reads a lot.

☐ She enjoys driving a bus.

☐ She is a loving mother.

☐ other _____

Prove It! What evidence in the play supports your answer?
Check the boxes. ✓ Make notes.

Evidence	Notes
☐ what Mrs. Nguyen says	
☐ what Mrs. Nguyen does	
☐ the illustrations	
☐	

Write About It!

CONCLUSIONS AND GENERALIZATIONS

Answer question **2** **using evidence from the text.**

_____

_____

_____

_____

_____

_____

condition
horrified
memorable
shortage
yearning

TALL TALES

People have always had a

1 _____ for entertainment.

In the past, there was no TV. So people

amused each other by telling stories. Folktales

are stories that have been passed along by

word of mouth.

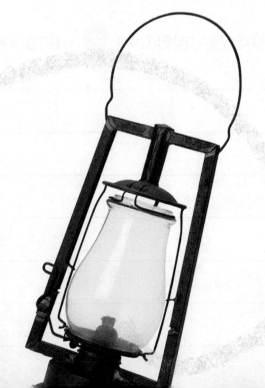

One type of folktale is the tall tale. Tall tales are often about frontier times. Some of these tales are **2** _____. You can tell because they've been told for a long time.

The heroes of tall tales are usually in great physical **3** _____. Tall tales often have characters that do amazing things.

There is no **4** _____ of humor in tall tales. Parts of the story are exaggerated to be funny. Tall tale heroes solve problems in ways that are hard to believe. You might be **5** _____ by the sight of a giant blue ox. People in Paul Bunyan stories are not scared of his ox, Babe. They're part of the tall tale, too!

6327

Babe's Vacation

by
Estelle Kleinman

Paul Bunyan was just a boy. He was a bit smaller than a stadium but a lot taller than a house. One winter, Paul found a blue ox in the woods. He named him Babe. Babe grew to be big and strong like Paul. When Paul became a lumberjack, Babe worked with him.

They worked really hard. They cleared big trees and little trees. Then, one day, they cleared the last tree on the Great Plains.

"Well, that's it for now," said Paul. "I think we both need a vacation."

Stop | **Think** | **Write**

How are Paul and Babe alike?

_____

_____

_____

"A vacation! How wonderful!" cried Bessie, Babe's wife. Their children, Belle and Blue, were excited, too.

"I've always had a **yearning** to tour the country," Bessie added.

Blue and Belle agreed. "Then that's just what we'll do," said Babe.

Their first stop was the Great Lakes. The family stopped off at each of the six lakes to splash around. When they got to the last lake, they were very thirsty. They drank and drank and drank. Soon the lake was empty. That's why today there are only five Great Lakes.

Stop | Think | Write

UNDERSTANDING CHARACTERS

Does Babe care about his family? Explain.

_____

_____

_____

The next stop was New York City. The tall buildings were just the right height for Blue to lean against.

"Stop that!" scolded Belle. "You'll scare the people." However, no one noticed. City people were in too much of a hurry to worry about big blue oxen.

The hefty oxen made many holes as they walked. Soon the ground was in poor **condition**. The mayor decided to use the holes to dig tunnels and run trains underground. That's how the subway system was born.

Stop   Think   Write

What have you learned about Belle?

_____

_____

_____

Next, the family went to Florida. Blue and Belle played in the waves. Their rough play turned the waves around. The waves got bigger as they went out to sea.

A hurricane was on the way. The big waves made it go back in the other direction. The children had saved the day!

"Let's go to Texas," said Babe. "Maybe we can help fix their water **shortage**." He hooked one of his horns onto a big rain cloud. Then he dragged it along with him. When it burst open, everyone in Texas enjoyed a nice cool shower.

Stop Think Write

VOCABULARY

What might cause a water shortage?

_____

_____

_____

The Rocky Mountains were the next stop.
"How lovely!" Bessie cried.

"Let's slide down the peaks!" called Blue.

"Be careful," said Bessie. They all agreed to watch their step. They took turns sliding down and tumbling into the riverbed below. It broke open a little more with each slide. Finally, it cracked wide open. This left big craggy walls and a path for the river to rush through. The riverbed was now the Grand Canyon!

Stop | Think | Write

Why does Bessie want her family to be careful?

_____

_____

_____

It was time to warm up again. Off the family went to California.

One morning, Bessie felt the ground shaking. **Horrified**, she woke up the others. They soon found a spot where the earth was moving in different directions.

"Here's the problem," said Babe. "Let's try to fix it."

Babe and Belle stood on one side. Blue and Bessie stood on the other. They pushed the ground back together. The rumbling stopped. That was the end of that earthquake!

Stop **Think** **Write**

STORY STRUCTURE

How does the family stop the earthquake?

_____

_____

_____

Soon it was time to go home. The oxen worked their way across deserts, mountains, and rivers. At last, they reached their farm.

The tired oxen settled down in their beds of straw. The door to the barn was open, and they could see the night sky.

"That was a **memorable** vacation," said Babe.

"Yes, we saw many fine things," said his wife.

"We did, but nothing is finer than the stars hanging over our home," Babe noted.

His family agreed.

Stop | **Think** | **Write**

VOCABULARY

Why is the vacation <u>memorable</u> for the family?

_____

_____

_____

Look Back and Respond

1 How does Babe show that he is thoughtful of others?

Hint

For clues, see pages 45, 47, and 49.

_____

_____

_____

2 How would you describe Bessie?

Hint

For clues, see pages 46, 48, and 49.

_____

_____

_____

3 Could anything in this story really happen? Explain.

Hint

Take a close look at the characters. Could they be real? Is anything they do possible?

_____

_____

_____

4 What makes this story funny?

Hint

Your answer to question 3 should help you.

_____

_____

_____

Be a Reading Detective!

Return to

"Stormalong"
Student Book pp. 139–153

1 **How do the sailors feel about Stormalong?**

- ☐ They admire him.
- ☐ They envy him.
- ☐ They fear him.

Prove It! What evidence in the story supports your answer?
Check the boxes. ✓ Make notes.

Evidence	Notes
☐ the story about the octopus	
☐ the sailors' actions when he returns from Kansas	
☐ the actions of *The Courser*'s crew	

Write About It!

UNDERSTANDING CHARACTERS

Answer question 1 using evidence from the text.

_____

_____

_____

_____

_____

_____

_____

2 **What lesson about life can readers learn from the story?**

- ☐ Being different can have both good and bad consequences.
- ☐ Sailors are the happiest people in the world.
- ☐ Slow and steady wins the race.
- ☐ other _____

Prove It! What evidence in the story supports your answer?
Check the boxes. ☑ Make notes.

Evidence	Notes
☐ what Stormalong does and says	
☐ what other characters do and say	
☐ the illustrations	
☐	

Write About It!

THEME

Answer question **2** using evidence from the text.

_____

_____

_____

_____

_____

_____

_____

51B

Lesson 6

✔ TARGET VOCABULARY

alarmed
awe
convey
extraordinary
fade

space, man

Check the answer.

1 After discovering a beautiful new planet, the scientist looked through his telescope in _____.

☐ alarm   ☐ awe   ☐ disgust

2 As the moon goes from its full phase to its new (dark) phase, its brightness begins to _____.

☐ fade   ☐ intensify   ☐ glow

3 It is hard to _____ the beauty of our planet as seen from space.

☐ remember   ☐ convey   ☐ fade

4 When the spaceship began running out of oxygen, the astronaut became _____.

☐ **alarmed** ☐ **extraordinary** ☐ **bored**

5 Newspapers around the world described Neil Armstrong's first walk on the moon as an _____ accomplishment.

☐ **awful** ☐ **alarming** ☐ **extraordinary**

6 Describe a time when you felt <u>extraordinary</u> at school.

_____

_____

_____

7 Describe a part of our solar system that leaves you in <u>awe</u>.

_____

_____

_____

THE SPACE FLIGHT SIMULATOR

By Justin Shipley

Characters: Jen, Kristen, Rachel, Phil—Director of the Observatory, Mingling Students

SCENE 1

Setting: Outside the space flight simulator at the Centerville Space Observatory in a crowd of students.

Phil: *(enters)* Hello, everybody! We hope you're ready for today's flight-simulator competition. The winners will be going to Space Camp.

Jen: *(squeezes best friend Kristen's arm)* Space Camp! Did you hear that, Kristen? We have to win!

Stop | **Think** | **Write**

STORY STRUCTURE

Who is the main character likely to be? What makes you think so?

_____

_____

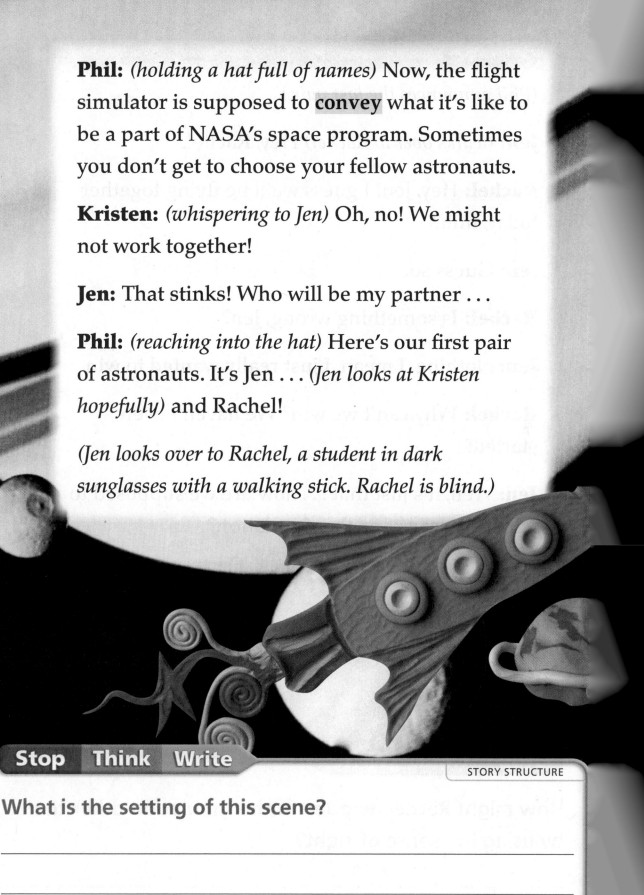

Phil: *(holding a hat full of names)* Now, the flight simulator is supposed to **convey** what it's like to be a part of NASA's space program. Sometimes you don't get to choose your fellow astronauts.

Kristen: *(whispering to Jen)* Oh, no! We might not work together!

Jen: That stinks! Who will be my partner . . .

Phil: *(reaching into the hat)* Here's our first pair of astronauts. It's Jen . . . *(Jen looks at Kristen hopefully)* and Rachel!

(Jen looks over to Rachel, a student in dark sunglasses with a walking stick. Rachel is blind.)

Stop **Think** **Write**

STORY STRUCTURE

What is the setting of this scene?

_____

_____

_____

(Phil announces the last pair.)

Jen: *(walks over to Rachel)* Hey, Rachel.

Rachel: Hey, Jen! I guess we'll be flying together today, huh?

Jen: Guess so.

Rachel: Is something wrong, Jen?

Jen: Nothing. I mean, I just really wanted to win.

Rachel: Why can't we win? We haven't even started!

Jen: Well, it's just that . . . how are we supposed to win if you can't see the simulation?

Stop | **Think** | **Write**

How might Rachel help Jen in the simulation other than by using her sense of sight?

_____

_____

_____

Rachel: There's more to a simulation than just sight, Jen. Astronauts use all five senses.

Phil: *(calls out)* Okay, Jen and Rachel! *(explains)* During the simulation you'll receive an emergency broadcast. Now don't be **alarmed**, but just like on real missions, the broadcast might get distorted. You'll have to use your best judgment to complete the mission.

Rachel: Don't worry, Jen. We'll win!

Jen: *(doubtful)* I hope so.

Stop   Think   Write

CITE TEXT EVIDENCE

At the end of Scene I, does Jen think she and Rachel will win the competition? How do you know?

_____

_____

_____

SCENE II

Setting: In the cockpit of the space flight simulator.

Rachel: Hey, we'll be great as long as we work together, okay?

Jen: You're right. I'm in! Set the boosters to full. It's the second button on your right.

Rachel: *(feels the buttons and presses one)* Got it!

Phil: *(speaking on a video screen inside the simulator)* Emergency! . . . must refuel! Head to the Space Station . . . on . . . quadrant . . . sector . . .

Jen: *(panicked)* Rachel, I can't understand what he's saying! I don't know where to refuel!

Stop Think Write

Where does Scene II take place? How do you know?

_____

_____

_____

Rachel: *(listens intently)* Shhh . . . quiet! Let me listen! *(after a moment)* Quadrant six, sector two!

Jen: Are you sure?

Rachel: Positive!

Jen: Heading to quadrant six, sector two!

(Jen punches in the coordinates.)

Phil: *(on screen)* Congratulations, astronauts, you saved the ship and got a new high score!

*(Jen looks at Rachel in **awe**.)*

Stop · Think · Write

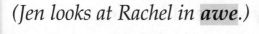

VOCABULARY

What does Rachel do that makes Jen feel <u>awe</u> toward her?

_____

_____

_____

SCENE III

Setting: Outside the space flight simulator.

Jen: *(loudly, to be heard over cheering students)* Rachel, how did you know where to refuel? I couldn't understand the message at all!

Rachel: *(loudly)* I spend so much of my life listening, I just knew what the message meant!

Jen: I'm sorry I ever doubted you, Rachel. I would never have known where to refuel without your **extraordinary** sense of hearing.

Rachel: I couldn't have done it without you.

Jen: Space Camp, here we come!

(Fade lights.)

Stop Think Write

THEME

How do Jen's feelings about Rachel and her abilities change at the end of the play?

_____

_____

_____

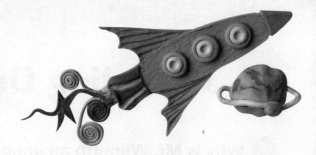

Look Back and Respond

1 Why is Jen disappointed to find out Rachel is her partner?

Hint

For a clue, see page 55.

_____

_____

_____

2 In Scene II, is Phil inside the cockpit with Rachel and Jen? How do you know?

Hint

For a clue, see page 58.

_____

_____

3 What is the most exciting part of the play?

Hint

Think about what happens on pages 58 and 59.

_____

_____

_____

4 How do you know Rachel's hearing is extraordinary?

Hint

For clues, see pages 59 and 60.

_____

_____

_____

Be a Reading Detective!

Return to

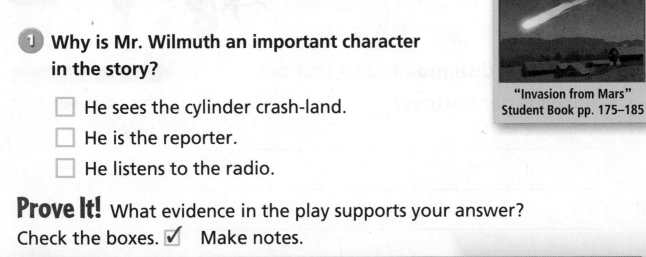

INVASION from MARS
a radio play by Howard Koch
illustrated by JT Morrow

"Invasion from Mars"
Student Book pp. 175–185

1 **Why is Mr. Wilmuth an important character in the story?**

☐ He sees the cylinder crash-land.

☐ He is the reporter.

☐ He listens to the radio.

Prove It! What evidence in the play supports your answer? Check the boxes. ☑ Make notes.

Evidence	Notes
☐ what the reporter says	
☐ what Mr. Wilmuth says	
☐ the illustrations	

Write About It!

STORY STRUCTURE

Answer question **1** using evidence from the text.

_____

_____

_____

_____

_____

_____

_____

2 Do you think Mr. Phillips is a good reporter?

☐ yes   ☐ no

☐ There is not enough evidence.

☐ other _____

Prove It! What evidence in the play supports your answer? Check the boxes. ☑ Make notes.

Evidence	Notes
☐ how Mr. Phillips speaks to other characters	
☐ how Mr. Phillips speaks to radio listeners	
☐ the illustrations	

Write About It!

UNDERSTANDING CHARACTERS

Answer question **2** using evidence from the text.

_____

_____

_____

_____

_____

_____

_____

_____

✓ **TARGET VOCABULARY**

angles
entertaining
focus
target
thrilling

Making Movies

1 It takes a big team to make an **entertaining** movie. First, the team needs a story. It has to be about something many people would like to see.

What is the most entertaining movie you have ever seen? Why?

_____

_____

2 Producers get the money to make a movie. They also set a **target** date for when it will come out. The movie might open on a holiday. More people go to the movies then.

Tell about a time you set a <u>target</u> date for something to be done.

_____

_____

_____

3 Directors decide what they want to stand out in a movie. They may **focus** on exciting action. They may stress how people grow and change.

What do you <u>focus</u> on in your free time?

_____

_____

4 The most **thrilling** scenes in an action movie may use stunt people. That way the stars of the film do not get hurt!

What is a synonym for <u>thrilling</u>?

_____

5 Sometimes the same scene can be shot from many **angles**, or points of view. The director chooses the best shots to be in the movie.

Describe an object in the classroom from two different <u>angles</u>.

_____

_____

_____

Film Facts

by Shirley Granahan

Have you ever wondered how movies are made? I have. So last summer I decided to find out.

Director Diego Gamba was in town. He was making his next film, *Holiday at Home*. I had a chance to visit Diego on the set.

Stop | **Think** | **Write**

MAIN IDEAS AND DETAILS

Where did the author meet Diego Gamba?

_____

_____

_____

"How do you get the ideas for your films?" I asked. "They are always so entertaining."

"I read a lot of stories," Diego said. "First, I target my audience. I decide if I want to make a film for little children, families, teens, or older people. Then, I pick a story I think the group will like. I figure out how to tell the story to my chosen audience."

Stop Think Write

VOCABULARY

The author says that Diego's films are <u>entertaining</u>. Is that a fact or an opinion? How do you know?

_____

_____

_____

Diego said directors must **focus** on one scene at a time. They must decide how each part of the story should look on film. "First, I break down the story into tiny parts," Diego said. "Next, I make a storyboard. It shows step by step how each part should look. Then, I plan ways to film each part."

Stop **Think** **Write**

MAIN IDEAS AND DETAILS

Why does a director make a storyboard?

_____

_____

_____

Directors also decide where to make a movie. They may film outside, in real places. They may build sets and film inside a building. They may even have actors work in front of a blue or green screen. Then computer pictures of places and things are added. So we may see a **thrilling** shot on a mountain top. It could be a real place or it could be movie magic.

Stop Think Write

VOCABULARY

How can computers help to make a movie shot thrilling?

_____

_____

_____

I also met Sara, the director of photography. "What do you do?" I asked.

"I run the cameras and lights," Sara said. "It is up to me to always get the best shot. So I shoot from different **angles,** or positions, around the set. I have to make sure the lighting is just right. It helps set the mood or feeling of a movie."

Stop **Think** **Write**

VOCABULARY

Why does Sara take pictures from different angles?

_____

_____

_____

"We pick the best actors for the story," said Diego. "They come to the set early. They put on costumes and makeup. Then we practice a scene before we shoot it."

"Movie scenes are short. To get it right, we may shoot the same scene many times," said Sara. "On a good day, we only shoot about three pages of the script."

Stop | **Think** | **Write**

CAUSE AND EFFECT

Why do the actors come to the set early?

_____

_____

_____

"Once we film all the scenes, we edit," said Diego. "That means we put together the best shots from each scene in the right order. We add sound effects and music. At last, it is a movie! Then we put it out and hope people like it."

Well, now I know how movies are made. I know Diego's new movie will be a big hit!

Stop **Think** **Write**

SUMMARIZE

What does it mean to edit a movie?

_____

_____

_____

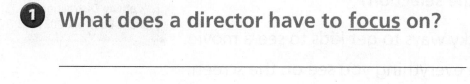
Look Back and Respond

1 **What does a director have to <u>focus</u> on?**

_____

_____

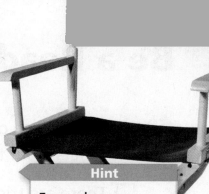

Hint
For a clue, see page 66.

2 **What does a director of photography do?**

_____

_____

_____

Hint
For a clue, see page 68.

3 **Why are so few pages of a script filmed each day?**

_____

_____

_____

Hint
For a clue, see page 69.

4 **Which sentence on page 70 tells an opinion?**

_____

_____

_____

Hint
Think about what an opinion is.

Be a Reading Detective!

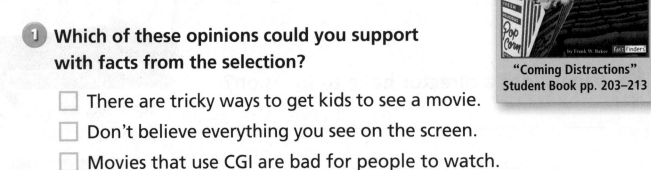

Return to

COMING
DISTRACTIONS
Questioning
Movies

by Frank W. Baker Fact Finders

"Coming Distractions"
Student Book pp. 203–213

1 **Which of these opinions could you support
with facts from the selection?**

☐ There are tricky ways to get kids to see a movie.

☐ Don't believe everything you see on the screen.

☐ Movies that use CGI are bad for people to watch.

Prove It! What evidence in the selection supports your answer?
Check the boxes. ✓ Make notes.

Evidence	Notes
☐ details from the text	
☐ clues in headings and captions	
☐ the photographs	

Write About It!

FACT AND OPINION

Answer question **1** using evidence from the text.

_____

_____

_____

_____

_____

_____

_____

2 What was the author's purpose for writing this selection?

- ☐ just to give facts and information
- ☐ to persuade people by giving facts and examples
- ☐ to tell an entertaining, made-up story
- ☐ other _____

Prove It! What evidence in the selection supports your answer?
Check the boxes. ☑ Make notes.

Evidence	Notes
☐ details about making movies	
☐ the author's advice at the end of the selection	
☐ the photographs	

Write About It!

AUTHOR'S PURPOSE

Answer question **2** using evidence from the text.

_____

_____

_____

_____

_____

_____

_____

Lesson

8

✓ **TARGET VOCABULARY**

concerned
glorious
ruined
schedule
studio

Murals

A mural is a wall painting. Many **glorious** murals have been painted. We can still see some that were painted long ago. One of them is in Rome. It is on the ceiling of the Sistine Chapel.

Some artists are **concerned** about the way their communities look. They want to brighten up their neighborhoods. One way to do that is by painting murals.

When artists create a mural, the city becomes their **studio**. A building or park wall is their canvas. The mural may take a lot of time to complete. Artists set up a **schedule** to make sure the project gets done.

Outdoor murals should be painted on clear, sunny days. They can be **ruined** if it rains before they are dry.

1 An artist who paints murals may use the city as a _____ .

2 Some artists are _____ about the way their communities look.

3 An outdoor mural can be _____ if it rains before it is dry.

4 Artists need to set up a _____ when they are working on a project.

5 There is a _____ mural on the ceiling of the Sistine Chapel.

6 What is your <u>schedule</u> like on Mondays?

_____

_____

_____

7 Have you ever had a project that was <u>ruined</u>? Explain.

_____

_____

_____

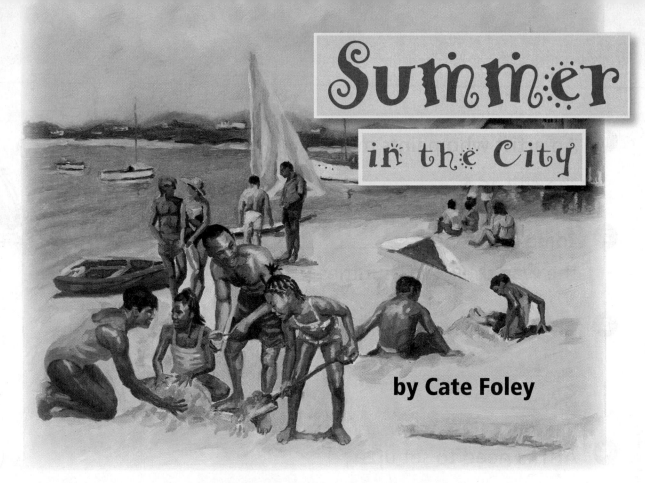

Summer
in the City

by Cate Foley

It was that **glorious** time of year again. Summer was finally here! Usually Joy couldn't wait for summer to begin. She loved to spend endless days at the beach swimming and sailing. Summers also meant a visit from her cousin Celia. Celia came from the city every year to visit. But this year Joy's summer **schedule** would be very different.

Stop **Think** **Write**

VOCABULARY

What activities normally make up Joy's summer schedule?

_____

_____

_____

This summer, there would be no beach for Joy. She would be spending her time in the city with Celia. What would she do there? How would she have fun away from the beach? Joy's summer would be **ruined**, she just knew it.

She tried to convince her mom that it was a bad idea. But her mother assured Joy that she would have a great time.

Stop	**Think**	**Write**	VOCABULARY

Why does Joy think her summer will be <u>ruined</u>?

_____

_____

_____

Joy arrived in the city and unpacked. The girls went to sit in front of Celia's building. "Do you just sit on the steps every day?" asked Joy.

"I like to sit outside. It's fun to watch people," said Celia.

Joy didn't think it was fun just to sit on the steps. "At my house, we can swim and sail," she said.

"We have fun in the city, too. But we do different things," said Celia. "You have to get used to things here. Then you might like the city."

Joy was **concerned**. She thought it was going to be a long summer.

Stop **Think** **Write**

UNDERSTANDING CHARACTERS

Why do you think Celia likes to watch people?

_____

_____

_____

The next day, Celia took Joy to the Youth Center. Celia was excited for Joy to see the art **studio**. She wanted Joy to join in on all the fun activities.

Ms. Howard was the group leader. She told the children stories about important African Americans. She said each child would make a poster of his or her favorite person. Joy smiled. Maybe this art class wouldn't be so bad.

Stop | Think | Write

Why do you think Celia is excited for Joy?

_____

_____

_____

All week long, Joy and Celia were glued to books about famous African Americans. They learned about Frederick Douglass, who fought against slavery. They read about musicians such as Duke Ellington. They discovered the writer Toni Morrison. Joy and Celia each picked a person for their posters. Joy couldn't wait to get started.

The next week, the girls headed back to the center. When they arrived, their mouths dropped open. They could not believe what they saw.

Stop **Think** **Write**

What does the author mean when she says, "Joy and Celia were glued to books about famous African Americans"?

_____

_____

_____

There was a crowd of people in front of the center.

"What's going on?" asked Celia.

"Someone wrote all over the walls!" said Ms. Howard.

"That's awful!" said Celia. "What should we do?"

"We could paint the walls," someone suggested.

"Someone would just write on them again," said Ms. Howard.

"I have an idea," said Joy. "We could paint a mural of important African Americans. It will be hard to write on the walls if there's a mural there."

Stop | **Think** | **Write**

CONCLUSIONS AND GENERALIZATIONS

How do you think the community members felt when they saw what had happened at the Youth Center?

_____

_____

_____

Everyone liked Joy's idea. They decided which people they would paint. Then they planned where each face would go. They drew sketches on the wall. Finally, they painted the pictures. Joy and Celia felt very proud as they worked.

When they were finished, the Youth Center looked even better than it did before. Celia and Joy hugged each other. But then a look of sadness came over Joy's face. "I leave in two days. I can't believe how fast the summer went. I can't wait to come back again next summer!"

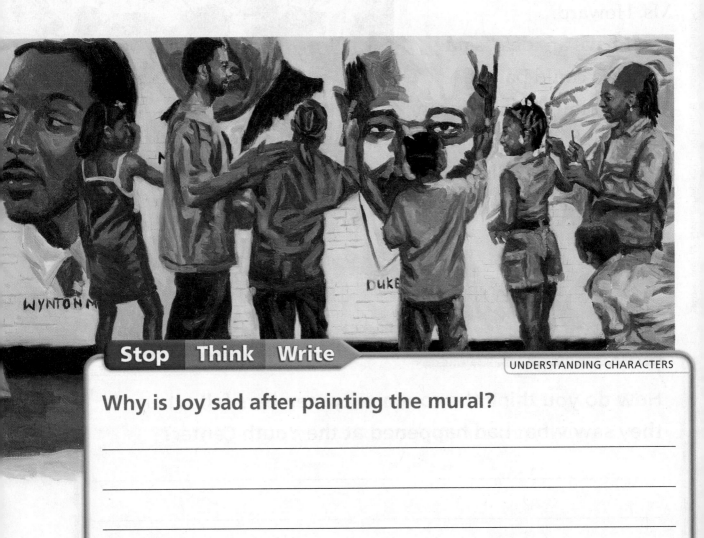

Stop | **Think** | **Write**

UNDERSTANDING CHARACTERS

Why is Joy sad after painting the mural?

_____

_____

_____

Look Back and Respond

1 Why is Joy <u>concerned</u> about spending the summer with Celia?

Hint
For clues, see pages 75 and 76.

_____

_____

_____

2 How is summer at the beach different from summer in the city?

Hint
For clues, see pages 75 and 76.

_____

_____

_____

3 How would you describe Joy?

Hint
Think about what Joy does and what she says.

_____

_____

4 Do you think the people at the Youth Center would want Joy to visit again next summer? Explain.

Hint
Clues can be found on pages 79 and 80.

_____

_____

_____

Be a Reading Detective!

1 **Think about the characters in this story.** Which character or characters would you describe as being kind?

- ☐ just Aunt Nanette
- ☐ just Uncle Romie
- ☐ both Aunt Nanette and Uncle Romie

Prove It! What evidence in the story supports your answer?
Check the boxes. ✓ Make notes.

Evidence	Notes
☐ what Aunt Nanette says and does	
☐ what Uncle Romie says and does	
☐ what James thinks, says, and does	
☐ the illustrations	

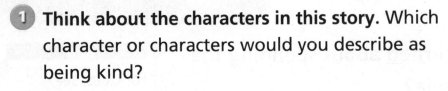

Write About It!

UNDERSTANDING CHARACTERS

Answer question **1** using evidence from the text.

_____

_____

_____

_____

_____

_____

2 **Why is Harlem important to the characters?**

Choose one or more answers.

☐ It is new and exciting for James.

☐ It is an important part of Uncle Romie's art.

☐ The setting is not very important.

☐ other _____

Prove It! What evidence in the story supports your answer?
Check the boxes. ☑ Make notes.

Evidence	Notes
☐ what James thinks, says, and does	
☐ what other characters say and do	
☐ the illustrations	

Write About It!

Answer question **2** using evidence from the text.

_____

_____

_____

_____

_____

_____

_____

apologize
borrow
genuine
insisted
slimy

Pet Snakes

Choosing a pet is tough. You should pick the type of animal that suits you best. My pet store owner **1** _____ that there is a type of pet for everyone.

For some people, a pet snake is perfect. It does not eat very often and requires very little care. Many people think that snakes are **2** _____, but they are not.

You should make sure to keep a snake's cage shut tight. If not, you might have to **3** _____ to your parents. They would not be happy about having a snake on the loose.

Snakes are cold-blooded. They need an outside source of heat to keep their bodies warm. You should keep the tank near a sunny window or a heater. You could also buy or **4** _____ a heat lamp for your pet.

Some snakes can be dangerous. You should not get a snake that is venomous. If a pet shop owner tells you a rattlesnake or a viper is a safe pet, he is not being **5** _____.

Snake Hunt
by Carol Alexander

Mr. Brown's class had a new pet. On Monday, Mr. Brown brought in a snake in a box. It was a small, striped snake.

"This little fellow is a garter snake," the teacher told the class. "He is not venomous. Let's take a closer look at him."

Kai wanted to touch him. Rita did not, though. She asked, "Is he slimy?"

Stop **Think** **Write**

CONCLUSIONS AND GENERALIZATIONS

How does Rita feel about snakes? Explain.

_____

_____

_____

"No, not really. Would you like to touch him?" asked Mr. Brown.

Rita slowly put out her hand. "Oh, he feels smooth and cool!" She smiled. "I have to **apologize** to you, Mr. Snake," Rita told him. "You're really pretty cute."

The next day all of the students wanted to see the snake again. However, he was not in his tank. The screen over the tank had been knocked off.

Stop | Think | Write

VOCABULARY

Why does Rita apologize to the garter snake?

_____

_____

_____

Tonya was very worried. "What could have happened to our snake?"

"Did someone **borrow** him?" Vic wondered.

Mr. Brown shook his head. "He must have gotten out of his tank—the screen has been moved. Please don't tell anyone else our wild critter is missing. We don't want to frighten anyone."

Just then, Maggie was passing by the classroom. "Wild critter!" she said aloud. "*What* critter?"

James thought he heard the word "cougar." He ran down the hall, yelling, "There's a cougar on the loose! That's one dangerous wild cat!"

Stop **Think** **Write**

CONCLUSIONS AND GENERALIZATIONS

What makes James believe a dangerous animal is in the building?

_____

_____

_____

Alex thought James was saying "cobra." "Ooh, cobras are deadly snakes!"

All this time, Mr. Brown's class was hunting for the garter snake. Kai and Vic peered into the closet. Rita and Tonya searched through the plants by the window. Where could the snake have gone?

"This is a real mystery," Mr. Brown stated, scratching his head. "When we find our snake, we'll put him back in the tank and make sure he stays in there. That's a **genuine** promise."

Someone knocked on the door loudly. Then a crowd of students ran into the room.

Stop | Think | Write

VOCABULARY

Why does Mr. Brown want the class to know his promise is <u>genuine</u>?

_____

_____

_____

"We heard about the cougar!" yelled James.

"They say you let a dangerous cobra get loose!" Alex cried.

"Where on earth did you hear that?" Mr. Brown asked in surprise. He **insisted** that everyone stay calm.

The rest of the class gathered around the teacher's desk. Kai pointed upward. "Mr. Brown, we didn't look everywhere after all. Just see what is on the top shelf!"

Stop **Think** **Write**

INFER AND PREDICT

What do you think Mr. Brown and the students see?

_____

_____

_____

There was the garter snake, curled up on the shelf.

"He doesn't look scary to me," Maggie said. "Are you sure that's a cobra?"

"It's a garter snake," Mr. Brown said. "Perfectly harmless."

"Not a cougar then," James sighed. He sounded disappointed.

Mr. Brown got a ladder and carefully lifted the snake off the shelf. "Heat rises," he explained. "Our pet may have been looking for a comfortable spot."

"What a day!" Kai exclaimed. "We lost a cougar and a cobra but found a garter snake."

Stop   Think   Write

CONCLUSIONS AND GENERALIZATIONS

Do you think snakes like to be warm or cool? What makes you think so?

_____

_____

_____

How Do Snakes Move?

Snakes have special muscles that help them move. These muscles are connected to their ribs. The scales on a snake's belly help it to move along, too.

The Farmer's Friend

Some farmers like snakes, as long as they aren't venomous. Snakes eat insects, mice, and rats. Without snakes around, the mice and rats eat up the crops of grain and vegetables. Garter snakes are friends of the farmer. So are ribbon snakes and rat snakes.

The Truth About Snakes

There are at least 2,500 kinds of snakes. About 400 kinds are venomous. Many snakes are harmless to people. In the U.S., there are only four types of venomous snakes. They are the rattlesnakes, copperheads, water moccasins, and coral snakes.

Stop **Think** **Write**

CONCLUSIONS AND GENERALIZATIONS

Is the copperhead a farmer's friend? Explain.

_____

_____

_____

Look Back and Respond

1 Why do you think Mr. Brown wants Rita to touch the garter snake?

Hint
For a clue, see page 85.

_____

_____

_____

2 How does the snake escape?

Hint
For a clue, see page 86.

_____

_____

_____

3 What might have happened if the rumors continued to spread around the school?

Hint
For clues, see pages 86, 87, and 88.

_____

_____

_____

4 Most snakes aren't dangerous. Do you agree or disagree? Explain.

Hint
For clues, see page 90.

_____

_____

_____

Be a Reading Detective!

Return to

"Dear Mr. Winston"
Student Book pp. 261–271

1 **Draw a conclusion.** Do you think Mr. Winston will come back to the library?

☐ yes   ☐ no   ☐ no way to know

Prove It! What evidence in the story supports your answer? Check the boxes. ☑ Make notes.

Evidence	Notes
☐ Mr. Winston's feeling about snakes	
☐ Mr. Winston's words and actions	
☐ the illustrations	
☐ the setting	
☐	

Write About It!

CONCLUSIONS AND GENERALIZATIONS

Answer question **1** using evidence from the text.

_____

_____

_____

_____

_____

_____

_____

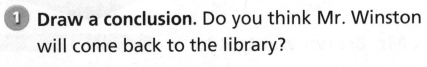

2 **The story is told from Cara's point of view.** What is she most concerned about?

☐ Mr. Winston   ☐ her snake   ☐ a book

☐ other _____

Prove It! What evidence in the story supports your answer?
Check the boxes. ☑   Make notes.

Evidence	Notes
☐ the illustrations	
☐ Cara's words and actions	
☐ Mr. Winston's actions	
☐	

Write About It!

POINT OF VIEW

Answer question **2** using evidence from the text.

_____

_____

_____

_____

_____

_____

_____

91B

**debut
discouraged
permission
toured
triumph**

Ballet

1 A ballerina has to study and practice for many years. She has to start learning to dance at a very young age and needs her parents' **permission** to go to ballet school.

What is an activity that you would need permission to do?

_____

2 After completing school, students who are not **discouraged** by the amount of work join a workshop. The best dancers are invited to join a dance company. Their careers as dancers have begun!

Tell about a hard job you have done in the past. How did you keep yourself from getting discouraged?

_____

_____

_____

3 A dancer's first professional performance is a **debut**. The way he or she dances in the debut is important. It shows the world what the dancer can do.

What sort of <u>debut</u> would an actor have?

_____

_____

_____

4 The Ballets Russes was a famous ballet company. It was formed in Paris by a Russian dancer. The company **toured** all over the world.

What is a synonym of <u>toured</u>?

_____

5 The company had **triumph** after triumph in Europe. Two of its most famous dancers were Vaslav Nijinsky and George Balanchine.

Tell about a moment of <u>triumph</u> that your favorite team or club enjoyed.

_____

_____

_____

Maria Tallchief:

A Life of Dance

by Carol Alexander

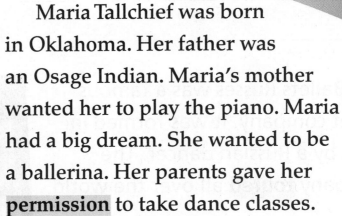

Maria Tallchief was born in Oklahoma. Her father was an Osage Indian. Maria's mother wanted her to play the piano. Maria had a big dream. She wanted to be a ballerina. Her parents gave her **permission** to take dance classes.

There weren't many dance schools near her town. Maria's parents saw how serious she was about dancing. The family moved to California, where they found good teachers.

Stop | Think | Write

CAUSE AND EFFECT

Why did Maria's family move to California?

_____

_____

_____

Following Her Dream

Madame Nijinska was a great dancer. She agreed to teach Maria. Maria was only twelve years old. She worked hard for many years. She had real talent. Her teacher knew Maria would go far.

When Maria finished school, she moved to New York City. She joined a dance company there. Maria made her **debut** with this company. Now people knew her name. Her dream was coming true.

Stop | Think | Write

VOCABULARY

What did Maria have to do before she could make her debut as a dancer?

_____

_____

_____

A Rough Road

Not everyone believed in Maria. However, she did not get **discouraged**. She knew the road could be hard. She kept right on working. Dance was her life.

One day, the company got a new leader. His name was George Balanchine. He knew Maria was a great dancer. He gave her big parts in his ballets. He created works just for her. People came to see this beautiful dancer. She won many fans.

Stop | **Think** | **Write**

VOCABULARY

Why might Maria have become discouraged?

_____

_____

_____

A Life of Dance

Maria **toured** cities around the world. She joined Balanchine's new company, the Ballet Society. She became the lead dancer. Now she was really a star!

Maria could express feelings with every movement. She made the hardest moves look easy. The fans loved her.

Later, Maria formed her own company. She led the company and also danced with it. She helped train new dancers. The company did well. Maria was proud of it.

Stop **Think** **Write**

INFER AND PREDICT

Why might Maria have wanted to form her own company?

_____

_____

_____

A Rich Life

Maria stopped dancing on stage when she got older. She kept teaching. She wanted to stay involved with dance. She was a fine teacher. She had had her **triumph** as a lead dancer. Now, she would train others. The dance world did not forget her. Maria won many honors for her work.

Stop | Think | Write

CAUSE AND EFFECT

Why did Maria teach dance?

_____

_____

_____

Her Own Steps

Maria Tallchief truly lived a life of dance. She led the way for other American dancers and was glad to help them. Dance was important to her.

Why is Maria Tallchief so special? She once said, "A ballerina takes steps given to her and makes them her own." That's just what Maria did.

Stop	Think	Write

AUTHOR'S PURPOSE

Why do you think the author uses Maria's own words?

_____

_____

_____

More About Ballet

Ballet is a kind of dance. This form of dance began over 400 years ago. A ballet can tell a story. Some ballets show a mood or feeling.

A Career in Dance

Maria Tallchief danced with the Ballet Russe for five years. She was a member of the New York City Ballet for 18 years. The New York City Ballet was first called the Ballet Society.

George Balanchine

Balanchine was born in Russia in 1904. He became famous for creating great ballets. He came to the United States and changed the dance world here.

Stop **Think** **Write**

THEME

How do these facts help you understand more about Maria Tallchief's life in dance?

_____

_____

_____

Look Back and Respond

1 Why do ballet dancers have to start learning ballet at such a young age?

_____

_____

_____

> **Hint**
> Think about how Maria became successful.

2 What do you think Maria Tallchief's greatest triumph was? Explain.

_____

_____

_____

> **Hint**
> For clues, see pages 97 and 98.

3 What was the author's purpose in writing this text?

_____

_____

_____

> **Hint**
> Think about the purposes for writing.

4 Tell about someone you know who worked hard.

_____

_____

_____

> **Hint**
> Think about people who have been determined to reach their goals.

Be a Reading Detective!

Return to "José! Born to Dance" Student Book pp. 289–299

1 **What was the author's purpose for writing this selection?**

☐ to give information about José Limón

☐ to tell funny stories about Limón

☐ to persuade readers that Limón was a great painter

Prove It! What evidence in the selection supports your answer? Check the boxes. ☑ Make notes.

Evidence	Notes
☐ details about Limón's childhood	
☐ details about his life in New York	
☐ details about his dancing	
☐ details about his paintings	

Write About It!

AUTHOR'S PURPOSE

Answer question **1** using evidence from the text.

_____

_____

_____

_____

_____

_____

_____

2 **What caused José Limón to become a dancer?**

☐ He had wanted to be a dancer since his childhood.

☐ He saw a dance concert.

☐ He learned to dance in California.

☐ other _____

Prove It! What evidence in the selection supports your answer?
Check the boxes. ☑ Make notes.

Evidence	Notes
☐ Limón's thoughts and actions	
☐ what other people said and did	
☐ the illustrations	
☐	

Write About It!

CAUSE AND EFFECT

Answer question ② using evidence from the text.

_____

_____

_____

_____

_____

_____

_____

✓ **TARGET VOCABULARY**

experience
rage
rapidly
source
whirling

TORNADO DANGER

1 A tornado is a windstorm. **Whirling** air reaches speeds of 110 miles per hour. Violent winds rotate around and around.

Write about something you have seen whirling around and around.

_____

_____

_____

2 **Rapidly** flying debris can crash through almost anything. Tree branches fly through windows. Even cars can speed through the air.

Name two things that move rapidly.

_____

_____

_____

3 Being in a tornado is a dangerous **experience**. If it happens to you, you will have to seek shelter in a safe place.

Name an <u>experience</u> you remember having when you were young.

_____

_____

4 Lightning can be a **source** of light that makes a tornado glow. The sun can also light tornadoes. They can have different colors from white to blue.

Name a <u>source</u> of light in your home.

_____

_____

5 Winds **rage** stronger and faster as a tornado grows smaller! They can rip up trees and fences. Their force is unbelievable.

Why might people go into a basement when a tornado starts to <u>rage</u>?

_____

_____

Strange Storms

by Jason Powe

Around the world, different kinds of places have different kinds of storms. Tropical places may have hurricanes. The central part of the United States is called "tornado alley" for the wild windstorms that are common there. But what kind of storm is a simoom? Where does a simoom happen?

Caught in a Simoom

A simoom is a local name for a sandstorm that is most common in the Sahara desert. Being caught in a simoom is an **experience** that is impossible to forget. Suddenly you see a dark cloud. The cloud is moving toward you. **Rapidly!** You say to yourself, "That cloud is way too low and way too dark." Then you understand. This twisting, **whirling** cloud is not cloud. It's a simoom!

Stop **Think** **Write**

MAIN IDEA AND DETAILS

What do you expect to read about throughout this selection? What do you expect to read about in the first section?

_____

_____

_____

In a simoom, sand and dust **rage** in the wind. Wind twists around like a tornado. People and animals find it hard to breathe. *Simoom* means "poison wind." The temperatures in a simoom are hot. The only simoom ever recorded in the United States reached 133 degrees. That was in Goleta and Santa Barbara, California, in 1859.

Twenty minutes after it starts, a simoom is usually over. But everything around you may have changed. A simoom can move an entire sand dune!

Stop | Think | Write

MAKE INFERENCES

Why might nothing look the same after a simoom?

_____

_____

_____

Not Another Haboob!

If you live in Khartoum, a large city in Africa, you have probably seen a haboob. Haboobs are common in the summertime in hot, dry areas. When temperatures cool suddenly, air is forced downward. Sand or dust gets pushed up into the air. It is carried in a big cloud on the wind. Most often, haboobs are kicked up by oncoming thunderstorms. Other causes are possible, too.

In Arizona, haboobs are most common from May to September. These sudden, dangerous storms kill about five people per year there. If you are caught in a haboob, it's no laughing matter! Find a safe place to wait until the storm passes.

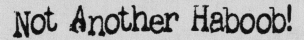

Stop | **Think** | **Write**

Why is a haboob dangerous?

_____

_____

_____

Black Blizzards

During the 1930s, a drought, or a very long period without rain, destroyed farmlands. "Black blizzards" raged across parts of the United States. These dust storms turned the sky black as they blocked out the sun. The areas most ruined by the black blizzards became known as the Dust Bowl.

Stop | Think | Write

CAUSE AND EFFECT

Why were these storms called "black blizzards"?

_____

_____

_____

The Dust Bowl

Raging sand and dust storms were the **source** of serious crop damage in the Dust Bowl. Dust and high winds damaged young plants. When it is very dry and the dirt is loose, the wind picks up soil and blows it away. Without soil, a field that once grew food can become a desert where nothing will grow. Thousands of families had to give up their farms on the American plains.

Stop **Think** **Write**

TEXT AND GRAPHIC FEATURES

What does the heading on this page tell you?

_____

_____

_____

Black Sunday

April 14, 1935, is known as Black Sunday. That is the day the worst black blizzard hit the Dust Bowl. Five million acres of wheat had already been destroyed by dust storms that year. This Sunday looked clear and safe in the morning. People went out to do chores or enjoy the fresh air. But in the afternoon, the temperature dropped fast. A huge black cloud appeared on the horizon. All at once, people were blinded by dust. People in their own backyards got lost trying to find the doors to their homes!

Stop | Think | Write

MAIN IDEA AND DETAILS

How was April 14, 1935, different from other days when there were dust storms in the Dust Bowl?

_____

_____

_____

Raining Frogs

Like simooms, haboobs, and black blizzards, it's wind that's to blame when this strange storm occurs. Very rarely, a waterspout—a storm like a tornado that forms over water—comes into contact with a community of frogs. Because frogs are lightweight creatures, sometimes, just sometimes, they can be drawn up inside a very strong waterspout.

When a waterspout moves from water onto land, it loses strength. Then the water, with whatever it has picked up, falls onto the land. It's quite unusual, but people have reported rains of frogs, fish, spiders . . . and even tomatoes! Can you imagine? Run for cover if you're caught in a tomato rain—or get a sauce pot!

Stop   Think   Write

TEXT AND GRAPHIC FEATURES

Write a caption for the picture on this page.

_____

_____

_____

Look Back and Respond

1 What do you think it is like to experience a sandstorm?

Hint

For clues, see pages 104 and 105.

_____

_____

_____

2 What is a common cause of haboobs?

Hint

See page 106.

_____

_____

_____

3 What kinds of storms happened in the Dust Bowl?

Hint

See page 107.

_____

_____

_____

4 What is another heading you could give to the section on page 110?

Hint

Reread the page and ask yourself what it is about.

_____

_____

Be a Reading Detective!

Return to

HURRICANES
Earth's Mightiest Storms

"Hurricanes"
Student Book pp. 321–329

1 **Page 324 includes a diagram of a hurricane.**
Which aspects of a hurricane does it show?

☐ its size

☐ how it moves

☐ what it's made up of

Prove It! What evidence in the selection supports your answer?
Check the boxes. ☑ Make notes.

Evidence	Notes
☐ arrows	
☐ distance and altitude numbers	
☐ labels	

Write About It!

TEXT AND GRAPHIC FEATURES

Answer question **1** using evidence from the text.

_____

_____

_____

_____

_____

_____

_____

2 **Is the following sentence a fact or an opinion?** Scientists have many ways to track and observe hurricanes.

☐ It is a fact.

☐ It is an opinion.

Prove It! What evidence in the selection supports your answer?

Check the boxes. ☑ Make notes.

Evidence	Notes
☐ photos of instruments	
☐ satellite images	
☐ text details about the photos and images	

Write About It!

Answer question 2 using evidence from the text.

_____

_____

_____

_____

_____

_____

Earthquakes

✓ TARGET VOCABULARY

debris
possessions
rubble
trembles
wreckage

1 During an earthquake, the ground **trembles**. The shaking movements can cause buildings and roads to collapse.

Write a synonym for <u>trembles</u>.

_____

2 An earthquake can leave **debris**. People must be careful not to hurt themselves.

Describe a time when you saw <u>debris</u>.

_____

_____

_____

3 In 1989, a road collapsed during an earthquake in California. People were trapped in the **wreckage**. Rescuers helped the people to get out.

What kind of <u>wreckage</u> might you find after a big storm?

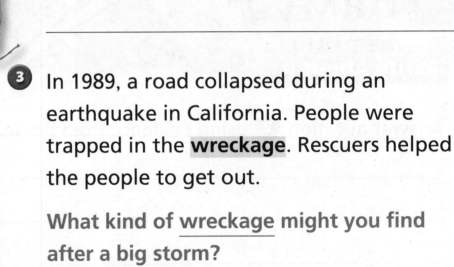

_____

_____

_____

4 A big earthquake hit Turkey in 1999. Buildings collapsed, and people were caught under steel and cement. Rescuers were able to get many out of the **rubble**. A little boy was found alive after 146 hours!

Why would it take a long time to move the rubble?

_____

_____

_____

5 After the earthquake in Turkey, many children lost their homes and **possessions**. Some groups worked to help earthquake victims. These groups replaced things that children lost.

What possessions would you mind losing the most?

_____

_____

_____

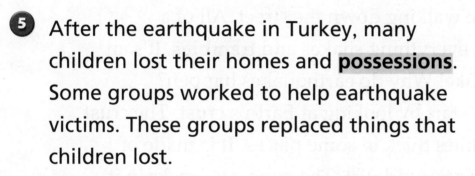

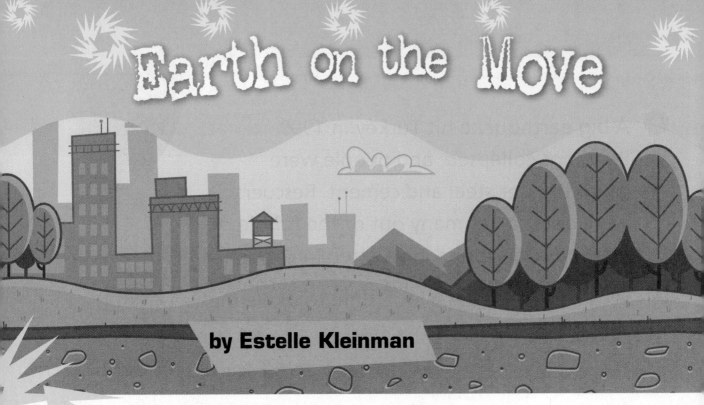

Earth on the Move

by Estelle Kleinman

Feeling the Earth Move

Have you ever felt the earth move? You might be walking down the street. All of a sudden, everything shakes and **trembles**. It's an earthquake! Why do earthquakes happen?

Let's start by looking at Earth's crust. The crust is fifty miles thick in some places. It is made of layers of rock and dirt. The crust has cracks in it. Over time, these cracks have divided the crust into big sections called plates. There are seven big plates and many smaller ones.

Stop | Think | Write

CAUSE AND EFFECT

What has happened to Earth's crust over time?

_____

_____

_____

Shifting Plates

The plates shift around. Much of the time they shift so slowly that you don't feel them move. It can take a year for the plates to move just an inch.

Heat from deep inside Earth makes these big rock plates rub and bump into each other. Cracks in the plates grow bigger. Then melted rock, which is called magma, can escape. This is called an eruption. Over time, magma from eruptions builds up. It can make new mountains.

Stop **Think** **Write**

SEQUENCE OF EVENTS

What must happen before magma under the plates can escape?

_____

_____

_____

115

Making Landforms

The plates press together in some places. They can twist and bend. One plate may slip under another. Big blocks of rock may rise or fall.

These shifting plates make many of the landforms we see. Blocks of rock can rise up to form mountains. Blocks can slip down to make valleys.

Stop **Think** **Write**

COMPARE AND CONTRAST

What is the difference between how plates move to form mountains and how they move to form valleys?

_____

_____

_____

Plates and Earthquakes

Plates usually shift very slowly. Sometimes they slip or crack all of a sudden. The result is an earthquake.

All earthquakes send out waves, like ripples on a pond. An earthquake can be so small that you can't feel it. A stronger earthquake sends out bigger waves. These can be felt for hundreds of miles. Strong earthquakes can harm people and animals. They can bring down trees and crack roads. Big buildings can also fall down, leaving nothing but **rubble**.

Stop | **Think** | **Write**

VOCABULARY

What other types of events in nature cause damage and leave rubble?

_____

_____

_____

Earthquake Records

Scientists keep records of earthquake waves. The records tell us where earthquakes happened and how strong they were.

Studying past earthquakes helps us guess where an earthquake may happen. Many happen where plates come together. Two big plates press together along the coast of California. Earthquakes often shake up this area. Some of the bigger ones can cause a lot of **wreckage**.

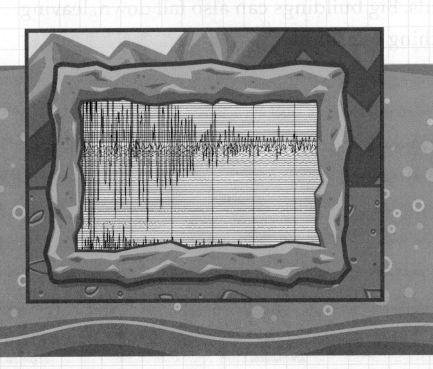

Stop **Think** **Write**

VOCABULARY

How do powerful earthquakes cause a lot of <u>wreckage</u>?

_____

_____

_____

During an Earthquake

What should you do when an earthquake starts? Stay calm. If you're outside, move away from things that can fall. Falling **debris** could hurt you.

If you're inside, think of your safety first. Don't worry about your **possessions**. You'll stay safe if you remember to drop, cover, and hold on. First, drop to the floor. Second, get under something for cover. Third, take hold of something strong.

Stop Think Write

SEQUENCE OF EVENTS

If you're inside, what is the first thing you should do when an earthquake strikes?

_____

_____

_____

After an Earthquake

After an earthquake, make sure that everyone is okay. You might smell gas or hear a hissing sound. If you do, it may mean that a gas line has cracked. Open a window and go outside.

You should be ready for a big earthquake. Put together a kit of things you may need. Your kit should have water, food, and a first-aid kit.

If you're scared, tell an adult how you feel. Earthquakes can be scary, but they last only a few seconds.

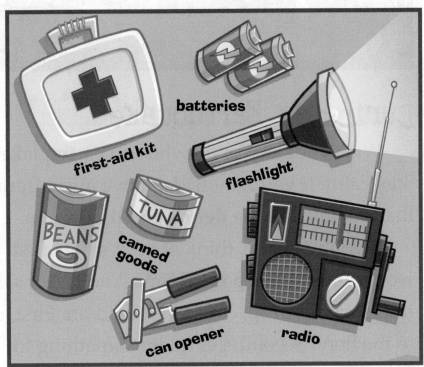

first-aid kit

batteries

flashlight

canned goods

can opener

radio

Stop **Think** **Write**

CAUSE AND EFFECT

What should you do if you smell gas or hear a hissing sound after an earthquake?

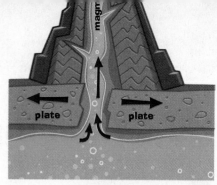

Look Back and Respond

1 What happens first: cracks form in the Earth's crust, or rock plates rub and bump into each other?

Hint
For a clue, see page 115.

_____

_____

_____

2 Name two things that can happen during a strong earthquake.

Hint
For clues, see page 117.

_____

_____

3 Why must "drop, cover, and hold on" be done in that order?

Hint
For clues, see page 119.

_____

_____

_____

4 What can scientists learn from studying past earthquakes? Explain.

Hint
For clues, see page 118.

_____

_____

_____

Be a Reading Detective!

Return to

THE
EARTH
DRAGON
AWAKES
The San Francisco Earthquake of 1906

LAURENCE YEP
Author of the Newbery Honor Books DRAGONWINGS and DRAGON'S GATE
Winner of the Laura Ingalls Wilder Award

"The Earth Dragon Awakes"
Student Book pp. 349–359

1 **What happens between 5:15 and 5:20 A.M.?**

☐ Ah Quon helps his neighbors.

☐ The ceiling collapses.

☐ The ground liquefies.

☐ Neighbors call "Fire!"

Prove It! What evidence in the story supports your answer?
Check the boxes. ☑ Make notes.

Evidence	Notes
☐ the time of day	
☐ the illustrations	
☐ events described in the text	

Write About It!

SEQUENCE OF EVENTS

Answer question **1** using evidence from the text.

_____

_____

_____

_____

_____

_____

2 **What problem is solved at the end of the story?**

☐ The fire is put out.

☐ Chin is rescued from the rubble.

☐ Chin's father is pulled out of the rubble.

Prove It! What evidence in the story supports your answer? Check the boxes. ☑ Make notes.

Evidence	Notes
☐ what Ah Quon does and says	
☐ what Chin does and says	
☐ the illustrations	

Write About It!

STORY STRUCTURE

Answer question 2 using evidence from the text.

_____

_____

_____

_____

_____

_____

_____

Lesson 13

✓ **TARGET VOCABULARY**

alert
display
huddle
stranded
weariness

122

Shipwrecks

Check the answer.

1 The captain of a ship must remain _____ for any signs of bad weather.

☐ **alert** ☐ **stranded** ☐ **tempted**

2 Some seamen have been _____ after shipwrecks that occurred close to land.

☐ **stubborn** ☐ **stranded** ☐ **pounced**

3 If sailors are shipwrecked in a cold place, they build fires or _____ together for warmth.

☐ **utter** ☐ **debut** ☐ **huddle**

4 Sailors can shoot flares or build a fire as a _____ of light to help others find them.

☐ **tenement** ☐ **display** ☐ **wreckage**

5 What is the first thing you would do if you were <u>stranded</u> on an island?

_____

_____

_____

6 Tell about a time when you experienced <u>weariness</u>. What made you feel this way?

_____

_____

_____

In the Grip of Ice

by Carol Alexander

Sir Ernest Shackleton was a British explorer. He wanted to do something that no one had done before. He wanted to cross the Antarctic by foot.

Shackleton put together a crew for the trip. Frank Hurley was the photographer. He would record the journey with photos. In the fall of 1914, Shackleton and his crew set sail for the Antarctic on the ship *Endurance*.

Stop | Think | Write

SEQUENCE OF EVENTS

What did Shackleton do before setting sail for the Antarctic?

_____

_____

_____

Anything for a Picture

Hurley carried his heavy cameras around with him. He remained **alert** for good subjects. The men said he "would go anywhere or do anything to get a picture." He even climbed up the masts of the ship with his bulky cameras. He stored the film on heavy glass plates.

As the ship sailed south, the crew came across penguins and seals. Hurley took pictures of these animals. It was amazing that there was life in such bitter cold!

Stop　Think　Write

Why did Hurley stay <u>alert</u>?

_____

_____

_____

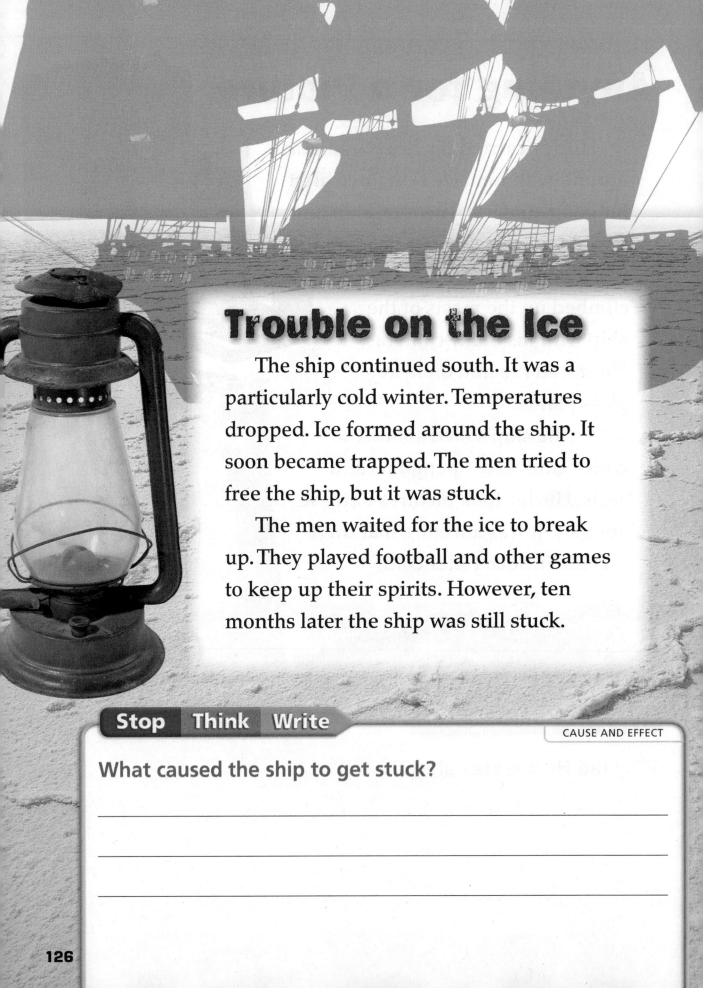

Trouble on the Ice

The ship continued south. It was a particularly cold winter. Temperatures dropped. Ice formed around the ship. It soon became trapped. The men tried to free the ship, but it was stuck.

The men waited for the ice to break up. They played football and other games to keep up their spirits. However, ten months later the ship was still stuck.

Stop | **Think** | **Write**

CAUSE AND EFFECT

What caused the ship to get stuck?

_____

_____

_____

Stranded!

The ice got thicker. It eventually crushed the ship. Hurley dived into the freezing water to save some of his plates. A few days later, the ship sank. The men were **stranded**.

Shackleton led his crew across the ice. They needed to find solid land. They dragged lifeboats with them. Hurley lugged his glass plates. The men had to **huddle** together to stay warm. Their clothes and sleeping bags were wet. They had little food.

Stop | Think | Write

VOCABULARY

What did the men do to survive when they were <u>stranded</u>?

_____

_____

_____

127

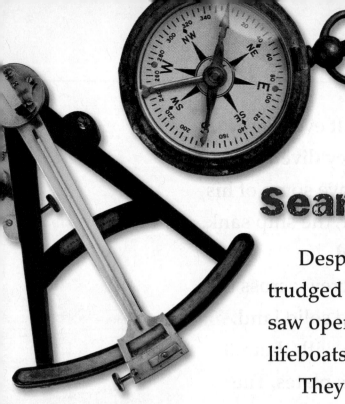

Searching for Help

Despite their **weariness**, the men trudged on. Months passed before they saw open water. The men sailed their lifeboats to Elephant Island.

They would not be able to survive there for long. Shackleton and five other men set sail in a lifeboat to get help. The trip was 800 miles. They traveled through storms for seventeen days. They chipped ice from the boat to keep it from sinking. They threw sleeping bags and spare oars overboard to lighten the load. Once they landed on South Georgia Island, they had to walk twenty-two miles over mountains to reach help.

Stop | Think | Write

SEQUENCE OF EVENTS

Did the men travel for long before they saw open water? What clue words help you to answer this?

_____

_____

_____

Saved!

Back on Elephant Island, the twenty-three men left behind were waiting to be rescued. Finally, on August 30, 1916, they saw a ship. It was Shackleton returning to rescue them. Four months had passed since he had left them.

All of the men had shown a **display** of true courage over the past two years. Not one person had died. Through all their hardships, Frank Hurley had captured their journey on film.

Stop Think Write

SEQUENCE OF EVENTS

Did the men on Elephant Island wait long for Shackleton to return? What was his return date?

_____

_____

_____

More About Ernest Shackleton and Frank Hurley

Before Frank Hurley became a photographer, he had many different jobs. He worked on the docks and at an ironworks. In 1911, he joined a crew bound for the Far North. It was his first big adventure.

Hurley's pictures from the trip to the Antarctic can be seen in the film titled *In the Grip of the Polar Ice Pack*. The film was first shown in 1919.

Ernest Shackleton first went to sea at the age of fourteen. His father thought the Navy would cure him of his love for the ocean! Instead, Shackleton spent much of his later life exploring the world by ship.

Stop Think Write

MAIN IDEA AND DETAILS

How do these facts add to your understanding of the story?

_____

_____

_____

Look Back and Respond

1 How is this text organized? Explain, using time clue words from the text.

Hint

Clues you can use are on almost every page!

_____

_____

_____

2 What caused Shackleton's crew to become stranded?

Hint

For a clue, see page 126.

_____

_____

_____

3 Was Shackleton a good leader? Explain.

Hint

Clues you can use are on almost every page!

_____

_____

_____

4 How did Hurley help people learn about the South Pole?

Hint

Think about what Hurley brought back.

_____

_____

_____

Be a Reading Detective!

Return to

Jennifer Owings Dewey

Antarctic
Journal
Four Months at the
Bottom of the World

"Antarctic Journal"
Student Book pp. 377–387

1 Which adventure comes next after falling into a crevasse?

- ☐ travel to Litchfield Island
- ☐ eating krill
- ☐ collecting a penguin egg
- ☐ seeing the green flash

Prove It! What evidence in the selection supports your answer?
Check the boxes. ☑ Make notes.

Evidence	Notes
☐ dates on journal entries	
☐ illustrations	
☐ events described in the text	

Write About It!

SEQUENCE OF EVENTS

Answer question **1** using evidence from the text.

_____

_____

_____

_____

_____

_____

_____

_____

2 How does the author inform readers about Adélie penguins?
Choose all the correct answers.

☐ text   ☐ photographs   ☐ sketches

Prove It! What evidence in the selection supports your answer?
Check the boxes. ☑ Make notes.

Evidence	Notes
☐ details about penguin behavior	
☐ photographs	
☐ sketches	

Write About It!

Answer question **2** using evidence from the text.

_____

_____

_____

_____

_____

_____

_____

Lesson 14

✓ TARGET VOCABULARY

excess
scarce
social
storage
transport

Interesting Insects

1 Termites are **social** insects. They live together in groups. Termites eat dead plants and wood. They recycle this material. This recycling helps the environment.

Do you like parties and other <u>social</u> events? Why or why not?

_____

_____

_____

2 Some people might think that there is an **excess** of beetles. There may be as many as 5 million different species of beetles!

Do you think it's possible to have an <u>excess</u> of friends? Explain.

_____

_____

_____

132

3 Some kinds of dragonflies are getting **scarce**. The wetlands that they live in are being destroyed. Fewer places to live means fewer dragonflies!

What things are <u>scarce</u> in your school?

_____

_____

4 The firefly is a kind of beetle. It has a special chemical in **storage** in its body. This chemical is used to make light.

What kinds of things might you put in <u>storage</u>?

_____

_____

5 Butterflies **transport** dustlike pollen from flower to flower. Pollen helps new flowers grow.

Which is the fastest way to <u>transport</u> people: by bus, by train, or by airplane?

_____

_____

Busy Bees

Honey for sale

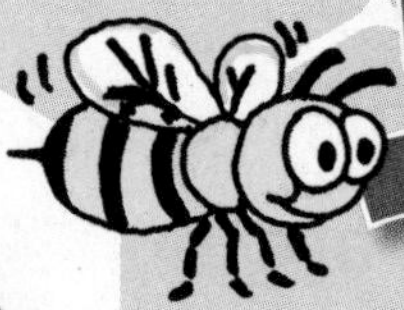

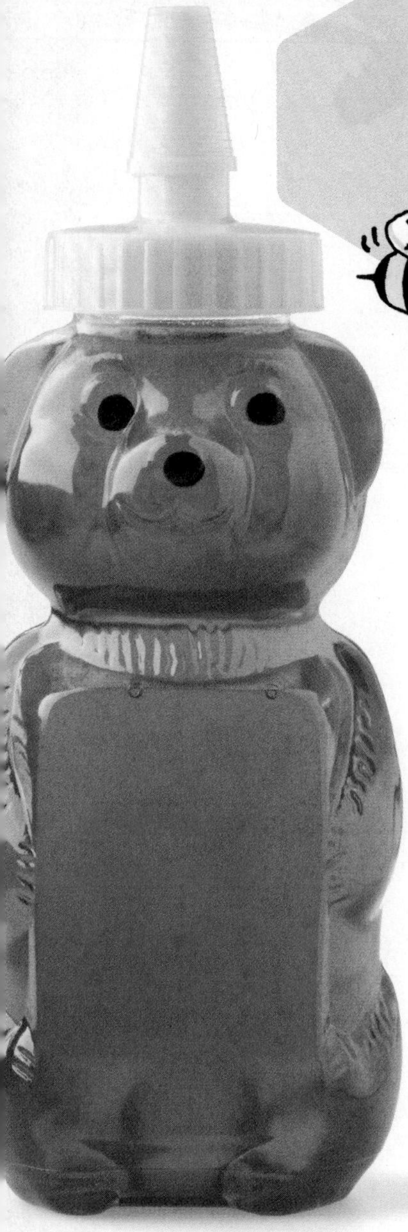

by Shirley Granahan

Do you like honey? I do. At school, we are learning where this sweet, sticky stuff comes from. Bees make it. But not all bees make honey. Only honeybees do.

We visited a honeybee farm, and we also saw movies about bees. We learned a lot about honeybees.

I used the information that I learned to write a report.

Stop Think Write MAIN IDEAS AND DETAILS

Where does honey come from?

____

____

____

The Bees' Home

We met the beekeeper at the farm. He told us that honeybees are **social** animals. They live and work together in groups. Thousands of bees live in just one hive.

We went to see a hive. There were so many bees, and they were all buzzing. Each bee has a different job to do.

Bees may live in hives like these.

Stop **Think** **Write**

VOCABULARY

Why are honeybees described as <u>social</u> animals?

_____

_____

_____

135

These cells are used to store honey.

The Bees in a Hive

Most of the bees in a hive are worker bees. The workers are all female. They build and care for the hive. They get the food. They take care of the baby bees.

Male bees are called drones. They are larger than the workers. Drones pick which baby bee will be the queen. The workers feed her royal jelly. It is sweeter than the jelly other bees eat. The queen grows much larger than other bees. It is her job to lay eggs in the cells of the hive.

Stop **Think** **Write**

MAIN IDEAS AND DETAILS

What types of bees live in a hive?

_____

_____

_____

The Honey in a Hive

The bees work together to make and store honey in the hive. They make sure that they always have enough honey in **storage**. In winter, they eat the honey. It gives them energy to live and work.

Beekeepers take **excess** honey from a hive. By taking only honey that the bees do not need, they make sure the bees will still have enough to eat.

The beekeeper collects honey.

Stop | **Think** | **Write**

MAIN IDEAS AND DETAILS

How much honey does a beekeeper take from the hive?

_____

_____

_____

Making Honey

Worker bees make honey. First, they fly to a garden filled with flowers. Then they buzz from flower to flower, drinking nectar. That is the sweet syrup found in flowers. Each bee stores some nectar in a part of its body called the honey stomach. Then the bees **transport** the nectar back to the hive.

Flowers provide bees with nectar.

Stop | **Think** | **Write**

CAUSE AND EFFECT

Why do honeybees fly from flower to flower?

_____

_____

_____

In winter, there are no flowers for bees.

The bees still have to turn the nectar into honey. They put the nectar into cells and take out extra water. Over time the nectar becomes honey. When the honey is ready, the workers make a cap over each cell.

The stored honey is the bees' only food source for the whole winter. If the honey starts to become **scarce**, workers push the drones out of the hive. Drones eat so much that they can drain the food supply.

That's the end of my report on bees.

Stop | Think | Write

VOCABULARY

Why does honey become <u>scarce</u> during winter?

_____

_____

_____

139

Bee Buzzings

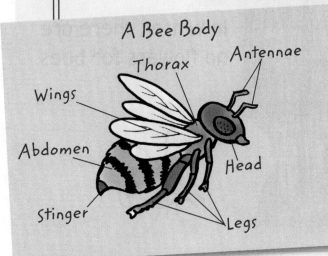

A Bee Body

Antennae

Thorax

Wings

Abdomen

Head

Stinger

Legs

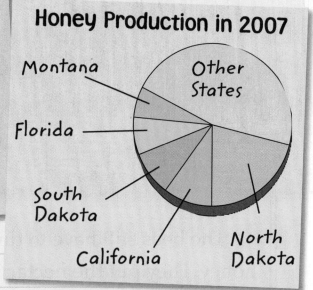

Honey Production in 2007

Montana

Florida

South
Dakota

California

Other
States

North
Dakota

A worker bee has different jobs in its lifetime.	
Age	Jobs
Days 1–3	Cleaning cells and taking care of eggs
Days 3–10	Feeding baby bees
Days 10–18	Wax making and cell building
Days 18–20	Guarding the hive
Day 20 and on	Gathering nectar and pollen from flowers

Stop **Think** **Write**

TEXT AND GRAPHIC FEATURES

A worker bee lives for six weeks in the summer. Which job does a worker bee spend most of its life doing?

Look Back and Respond

1 **Where do bees live?**

Hint

For a clue, see page 135.

_____

_____

_____

2 **What do bees do to make honey?**

Hint

For clues, see pages 138 and 139.

_____

_____

_____

3 **What would happen if a beekeeper took all of the honey from a hive?**

Hint

For clues, see pages 137 and 139.

_____

_____

_____

4 **Which state produced the most honey in 2007?**

Hint

Use the graph on page 140.

_____

_____

_____

Be a Reading Detective!

Return to

"The Life and Times of the Ant"
Student Book pp. 411–423

1 What features of a giant anteater help it gather and eat ants?

☐ black-and-white coloring

☐ four-inch-long claws

☐ long, sweeping tail   ☐ other _____

Prove It! What evidence in the selection supports your answer?
Check the boxes. ☑ Make notes.

Evidence	Notes
☐ drawing of giant anteater	
☐ caption about the claws	
☐ other captions	

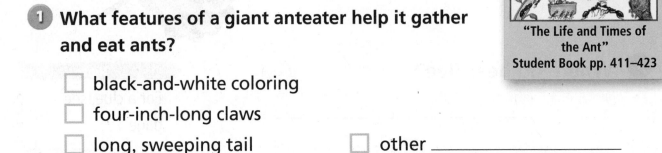

Write About It!

TEXT AND GRAPHIC FEATURES

Answer question **1** using evidence from the text.

_____

_____

_____

_____

_____

_____

_____

2 **What are two effects that leafcutter ants have on a jungle?**

☐ The jungle's overgrown trees are thinned out.

☐ The jungle has wide paths cut through it.

☐ The ants' recycled leaves help new plants grow.

Prove It! What evidence in the selection supports your answer?
Check the boxes. ☑ Make notes.

Evidence	Notes
☐ the main text about how ants recycle leaves	
☐ the diagram of leafcutter ants	
☐ captions on the diagram	

Write About It!

CAUSE AND EFFECT

Answer question **2** using evidence from the text.

_____

_____

_____

_____

_____

_____

_____

✓ **TARGET VOCABULARY**

affect
directly
habitats
species
traces

Frogs

Wetlands are **habitats** for frogs. Frogs thrive in moist, warm areas. Frogs can let you know about the health of their environment. They suffer **directly** from damage to wetlands.

Pollution hurts wetlands. It can **affect** frogs, too. One **species** of frog that has suffered is the wood frog. Many have died.

Scientists track frogs so they can tell how healthy an area is. They cannot see every frog. They look for **traces**. Frog calls are the best clues that frogs live in an area.

1. Scientists look for _____ of frogs to see how healthy an area is.

2. Moist, warm areas such as wetlands are _____ for frogs.

3. The wood frog is a _____ of frog that has suffered from changes to wetlands.

4. Do you go <u>directly</u> home after school? Explain.

   _____

   _____

   _____

5. What might negatively <u>affect</u> the environment in your area?

   _____

   _____

   _____

Where Have All the Frogs Gone?

by Cate Foley

Carlos was annoyed. He couldn't believe his mother had dragged him to one of her "save the planet" meetings. A baseball game was happening in the neighborhood. Carlos was the best center fielder on the block. Instead of making amazing catches, he was listening to some scientist talk about . . . frogs! Why was he here? What could he do to **affect** frogs? He was wasting his time.

Stop **Think** **Write**

INFER AND PREDICT

Why are people having a meeting about frogs?

_____

_____

_____

Dr. Vasquez had begun her talk about the frog population. She pointed to a bar graph on a screen. The graph looked like steps going down. Carlos could see the frogs were having a hard time surviving.

Dr. Vasquez explained that frogs are delicate creatures. Even **traces** of pollution could kill an entire population. People all over the world were helping to count frogs. Scientists held meetings. They taught people how to count frogs. Then people reported **directly** back to the scientists so they could keep track of information.

Stop **Think** **Write**

MAIN IDEAS AND DETAILS

What evidence does Dr. Vasquez give to show that frogs are delicate?

_____

_____

_____

One of the **habitats** Dr. Vasquez spoke of was a large wetlands area. It was right behind the baseball field where Carlos and his friends played. Carlos couldn't believe it was so close! He knew then that he wanted to help the frogs. He took notes while the room rang with trills and croaks. Dr. Vasquez was playing frog calls on a tape recorder.

Carlos left the meeting holding a frog-counting kit and photos of different frogs.

Stop **Think** **Write**

What happens when Carlos learns of the location of one of the <u>habitats</u>?

_____

_____

_____

The next evening was just right for frog counting. It was damp and warm with no wind. Carlos and his mother walked to the wetlands behind the baseball field.

They sat near the muddy pond that Dr. Vasquez had marked on the map. They took care not to damage the land. They were very still and quiet.

Stop **Think** **Write**

MAIN IDEAS AND DETAILS

What details show that the area Carlos and his mother visit is a good habitat for frogs?

_____

_____

_____

Suddenly, Carlos saw a streak of green. He heard a *plop!* It must have been a frog. Dr. Vasquez had said there were no fish in the pond. Something resembling a foghorn sounded from the middle of the pond. "Bullfrog," Carlos whispered and wrote it in his log.

Then Carlos heard a quacking call. The quacks came faster and faster, from a log nearby. "It might be a wood frog," Carlos thought. He held up a tape recorder. He hoped the microphone captured the frog's calls.

Stop | **Think** | **Write**

How does Carlos identify the frogs?

_____

_____

_____

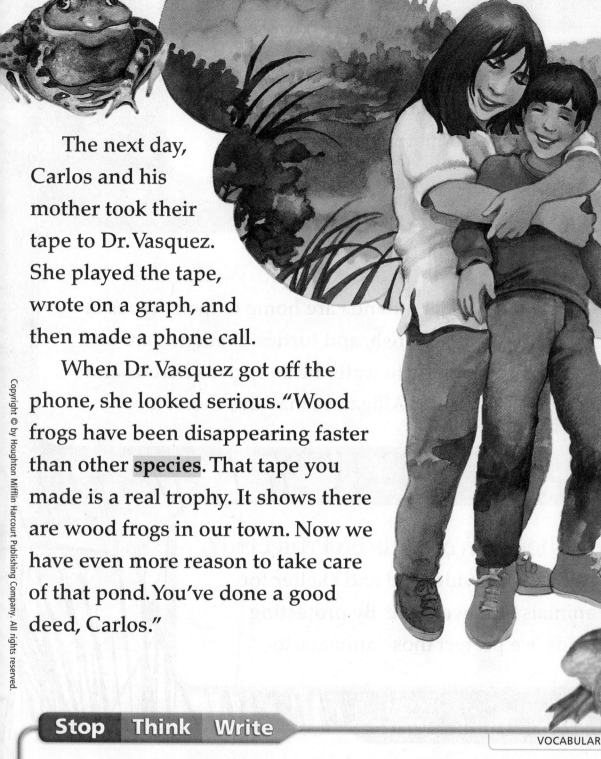

The next day, Carlos and his mother took their tape to Dr. Vasquez. She played the tape, wrote on a graph, and then made a phone call.

When Dr. Vasquez got off the phone, she looked serious. "Wood frogs have been disappearing faster than other **species**. That tape you made is a real trophy. It shows there are wood frogs in our town. Now we have even more reason to take care of that pond. You've done a good deed, Carlos."

Stop **Think** **Write**

VOCABULARY

What two <u>species</u> of frogs does Carlos observe at the pond?

_____

_____

_____

Where Wetlands Can Be Found

Wetlands can be found near lakes, ponds, and rivers throughout the United States.

What Lives in the Wetlands?

Wetlands are home to many types of frogs, fish, and turtles. Wetlands are also home to water birds such as herons and gulls. Alligators may live there, too.

Why Should Wetlands Be Protected?

Wetlands provide food and shelter for the animals that live there. By protecting wetlands, we protect those animals, too.

Stop **Think** **Write**

CONCLUSIONS

How do these facts help you understand why it is important to protect natural habitats?

_____

_____

_____

Look Back and Respond

1 **What details tell you that Carlos doesn't want to be at the meeting?**

> **Hint**
>
> For clues, see page 144.

_____

_____

_____

2 **How would you describe a wood frog's habitat?**

> **Hint**
>
> For clues, see pages 147 and 150.

_____

_____

_____

3 **What does Carlos learn about wood frogs?**

> **Hint**
>
> For clues, see pages 148 and 149.

_____

_____

_____

4 **What are some of the things you could do to help preserve frogs in wetlands?**

> **Hint**
>
> Clues can be found throughout the story.

_____

_____

_____

Be a Reading Detective!

Return to

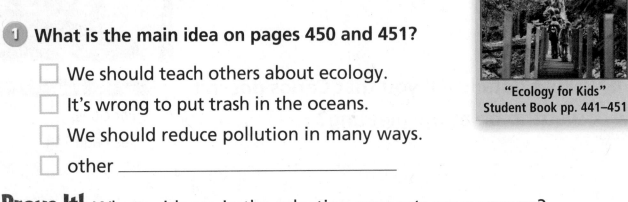

Ecology for Kids

"Ecology for Kids"
Student Book pp. 441–451

1 **What is the main idea on pages 450 and 451?**

☐ We should teach others about ecology.

☐ It's wrong to put trash in the oceans.

☐ We should reduce pollution in many ways.

☐ other _____

Prove It! What evidence in the selection supports your answer?
Check the boxes. ☑ Make notes.

Evidence	Notes
☐ the first sentence	
☐ details that support the first sentence	
☐	

Write About It!

MAIN IDEAS AND DETAILS

Answer question **1** using evidence from the text.

_____

_____

_____

_____

_____

_____

_____

2 **What is the author's purpose for telling readers about the resources people use from rain forests and from the sea?**

☐ to inform readers about some of his favorite sea animals

☐ to persuade readers that these resources are worth protecting

☐ to entertain readers with stories about forest adventures

Prove It! What evidence in the selection supports your answer? Check the boxes. ☑ Make notes.

Evidence	Notes
☐ the last sentence in each section	
☐ captions	
☐ persuasive words like *important*, *amazing*, and *should*	

Write About It!

AUTHOR'S PURPOSE

Answer question ② using evidence from the text.

_____

_____

_____

_____

_____

_____

_____

defended
relied
reputation
satisfied
situation

Wagon Trains

1 Each wagon train had a leader. Everyone on the wagon train **defended** the leader's right to make all the important decisions.

Write a synonym for <u>defended</u>.

_____

2 Most wagon trains **relied** on a scout to guide the wagons. Scouts knew the easiest places to cross rivers and mountains.

Tell about a time when you <u>relied</u> on someone to help you.

_____

_____

_____

3 One famous scout was Jim Bridger. People said that he "had the whole West mapped in his head." He had a good **reputation**.

What reputation would you like your school to have?

▲ **An elk**

_____

_____

_____

4 It was hard to find wood. Travelers sometimes used dried buffalo droppings. The droppings made a clean, hot fire. Travelers were **satisfied** that this was a good fuel.

Write a synonym for satisfied.

_____

5 The hunting **situation** changed from day to day. Sometimes hunters found only small animals. Farther west, they found elk.

In what situation did you feel proud?

_____

_____

_____

The Fastest Rider in the West

Special to *The Way West* by Nathan Mott

CONCLUSIONS AND GENERALIZATIONS

Based on the title, what event do you think Nathan Mott wrote about?

_____

_____

_____

The Way West is pleased to print part of Nathan Mott's journal. He wrote these pages to report on an exciting event along the Santa Fe Trail. We **relied** on Mott to follow a rider who is known as "The Fastest Rider in the West."

On the Santa Fe Trail—May 20, 1848

Here is my **situation**. I am standing in the middle of nowhere. Behind me is Independence, Missouri. Miles of grasslands lie ahead. I am hot on the heels of the fastest rider in the West, Francis Aubry. We left Independence, the start of the trail, at the same time. Now Aubry is ahead of me.

Stop **Think** **Write**

COMPARE AND CONTRAST

Who is a faster rider, Nathan Mott or Francis Aubry? Explain.

_____

_____

_____

Council Grove, Kansas—May 24, 1848

Today is Day Four of Aubry's ride. I'm here at Council Grove. Aubry has already left. All I found was his tired horse.

No horse can run at top speed for a long time. For this reason, Aubry has fresh horses waiting all along the trail. People keep the horses for him. When his horse gets tired, Aubry changes to another. Then he sets out again. That's how I'm traveling, too. To catch up to Aubry, I have to ride like him. I am not as fast as he is.

Aubry loves setting speed records. He has gained quite a **reputation**. His name is known all along the trail.

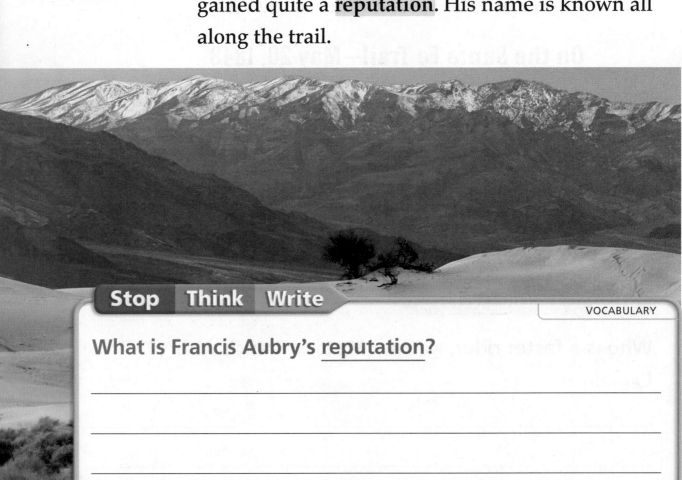

Stop | **Think** | **Write**

What is Francis Aubry's _reputation_?

_____

_____

_____

▲ **Wagon ruts along the trail**

Pawnee Rock, Kansas—May 26, 1848

It seemed like these grasslands would go on forever. Today, I reached the halfway point. I am now at Pawnee Rock.

Many travelers have carved their names in the soft stone here. Not Aubry. He would never waste time on that.

There is no sign of Aubry here. He must have left hours ago. Well, it's time to move on.

Stop | **Think** | **Write**

CAUSE AND EFFECT

Why do you think Aubry didn't carve his name into Pawnee Rock?

_____

_____

_____

Beyond the Desert—June 1, 1848

Will I ever catch up to Francis Aubry? I have ridden across the desert. I have crossed rivers, but I have not seen him.

Aubry doesn't travel like other people. They say he can get along on two hours' sleep. They say he can go without meals. They say he rode through mud in a terrible storm for twenty-four hours. A trader told me this was just a story, but I **defended** Aubry! I know how fast he moves. I know he's hard to catch!

VOCABULARY

Why do you think the reporter <u>defended</u> Aubry?

_____

_____

_____

Santa Fe, New Mexico—June 3, 1848

I have met Francis Aubry at last. I even shook his hand. He isn't a big man at all. He is strong and full of energy, though. I could have talked all day, but Aubry was in a hurry. He was on his way to meet with some traders. I shall have to be happy with just a short chat. I still can't believe that I was only one day slower than he was.

After the summer heat, Aubry will try another fast ride. He hopes to ride the trail in just six days. I am **satisfied** that Aubry can do it. Still, 800 miles is a long way to go in less than a week!

Stop | Think | Write

COMPARE AND CONTRAST

Who has more time to talk, Nathan Mott or Francis Aubry? Explain.

_____

_____

_____

Riding with Aubry

Life and Death

Francis Aubry was born in Quebec, Canada in 1824. He died in New Mexico at the age of twenty-nine.

How Fast Do They Travel?

Wagon train	Horse
2 miles an hour	20 miles an hour
15–20 miles a day	50 miles or more

The Fastest Ride of All

On Sept 12, 1848, Francis Aubry set out on his fastest ride of all. From Santa Fe to Independence: **780 miles, 5 days, 16 hours.**

Stop   Think   Write

COMPARE AND CONTRAST

Is it faster to travel by wagon train or by horse? Explain.

_____

_____

_____

Look Back and Respond

1 How are Nathan Mott and Francis Aubry different?

Hint
For clues, see pages 156, 158, and 159.

_____

_____

_____

2 What is one way that Mott's trip and Aubry's trip are the same?

Hint
For a clue, see page 156.

_____

_____

_____

3 How would you describe Aubry?

Hint
For clues, see pages 158 and 159.

_____

_____

_____

4 Is the ride in the story faster or slower than the six-day ride Aubry hopes to take after the summer? Explain.

Hint
Look at the dates on pages 155 and 159.

_____

_____

_____

Be a Reading Detective!

Return to

"Riding Freedom"
Student Book pp. 473–483

1 **How is life different for Charlotte after she loses her eye?**

☐ She gives up driving the stagecoach.

☐ She learns to depend on other senses.

☐ She loses the respect of her peers.

☐ other _____

Prove It! What evidence in the story supports your answer?
Check the boxes. ☑ Make notes.

Evidence	Notes
☐ what Charlotte figures out about driving	
☐ how Charlotte retrains herself	
☐ how Charlotte handles the stormy trip	

Write About It!

COMPARE AND CONTRAST

Answer question 1 using evidence from the text.

_____

_____

_____

_____

_____

_____

_____

2 **Which answer is true of Charlotte?**

☐ Charlotte is very dependent on others.

☐ Charlotte works for what she wants.

☐ Charlotte is afraid of change.

☐ other _____

Prove It! What evidence in the story supports your answer?
Check the boxes. ☑ Make notes.

Evidence	Notes
☐ Charlotte's response to her accident	
☐ the deal Charlotte makes	
☐ what Charlotte does in the storm	
☐	

Write About It!

UNDERSTANDING CHARACTERS

Answer question **2** using evidence from the text.

_____

_____

_____

_____

_____

_____

_____

✓ **TARGET VOCABULARY**

confidence
foster
patiently
performs
reward

Monkeys

Sometimes a monkey **performs** tricks in a circus. The monkey is like a tiny clown. It does tricks that make us laugh!

Many monkeys live in zoos with other monkeys. Some monkeys live in **foster** homes with people. The monkeys become part of the foster family.

Monkeys can mimic what they see. You can show a monkey how to shake hands. You'll have to wait **patiently**. The monkey will soon learn.

Monkeys love fruit. So people **reward** monkeys with treats such as grapes or oranges when they do something well. Of course, no monkey would turn down a banana!

Some tiny monkeys are trained to help people. The monkeys give people the **confidence** to do the things they want to do.

1 People _____ monkeys

with treats such as grapes or oranges.

2 Some monkeys live in _____

homes with people.

3 A monkey _____ tricks

in the circus and makes us laugh.

4 When are you expected to wait <u>patiently</u>?

_____

_____

_____

5 What could you do to give a friend the
<u>confidence</u> to try out for a role in a play?

_____

_____

_____

Monkey Business

by Shirley Granahan

What do you do if you drop something? You pick it up. What if you could not pick it up yourself? Who would give you a helping hand? Sometimes a monkey can help!

Stop | Think | Write

INFER AND PREDICT

In what situation would you not be able to pick something up?

_____

_____

_____

Helping Hands

Some people are not able to move their arms or legs. Some monkeys can learn to help. They can pick up things. They can open doors. They can turn lights on and off. They can even feed a person!

A tiny capuchin monkey makes a good helper. It can sit up on a person's shoulder. It can get into very small places. So it easily **performs** many jobs for people who need help.

Stop Think Write

VOCABULARY

A monkey <u>performs</u> many jobs. Which would be most helpful to you?

_____

_____

_____

Growing up with Humans

How does a monkey learn to help people? First, it must get used to living with people. So when a monkey is two months old, it moves into a home with a human **foster** family.

At first, a baby monkey can drink only from a bottle. Later, the baby monkey gets teeth. It begins to eat monkey food. It also gets snacks like grapes and oranges. A growing monkey loves to play. It likes to go places with the family. It likes to be hugged!

Stop | Think | Write

SEQUENCE OF EVENTS

What changes after the baby monkey gets teeth?

_____

_____

_____

Monkey School

The monkey lives with its foster family for about four years. Then it's time for school!

People teach the monkeys to follow orders. Some monkeys learn fast. Others may need more time. The teachers work **patiently** with each animal.

The monkeys work hard at school. They also have time to monkey around and have fun!

Stop Think Write

VOCABULARY

Why is working patiently important when teaching something new?

_____

_____

_____

167

Monkeys can learn to bring things to people. The teacher points a special light stick. A dot of red light shines on something. The monkey must get the thing and bring it back.

If the monkey does a good job, the teacher will **reward** it with a yummy treat! Soon the monkey learns to spot the dot every time. The furry helper brings the object back—even without getting a treat!

Stop · Think · Write

SEQUENCE OF EVENTS

What does the monkey have to do before it is rewarded?

_____

_____

_____

Off to Work

Now the teacher takes the monkey to its new home. The monkey and its owner learn to work together.

The monkey does many things to make life easier for the person. The person feeds and cares for the furry friend. The person has **confidence** that the monkey will always be there to help. The monkey has someone to hug for many years.

Stop **Think** **Write**

INFER AND PREDICT

Does the person or the monkey get the most out of this relationship? Why?

_____

_____

_____

Tiny Helpers

An Important Digit

Most animals don't have thumbs. Monkeys do! Thumbs help monkeys do many tasks. A monkey can even open a bottle.

Monkeys, Big and Small

Capuchin monkeys are very small. Some other monkeys are big. Mandrills are the biggest monkeys of all. They are not used for helping people.

Tasks a Monkey Can Do

- comb someone's hair
- put a straw in a drink
- put a CD in a player
- dial 911 on the phone

Stop | **Think** | **Write**

CAUSE AND EFFECT

Why can't a dog perform the tasks a monkey can?

_____

_____

_____

Look Back and Respond

1 Why do some people need monkeys?

_____

_____

_____

Hint
For a clue, see page 165.

2 Where does a monkey live before it goes to school?

_____

_____

_____

Hint
For a clue, see page 166.

3 What happens to a monkey after it has lived with its foster family for four years?

_____

_____

_____

Hint
For a clue, see page 167.

4 What other jobs do you think a monkey might do to help people?

_____

_____

_____

Hint
Think about times that you could use a helping hand!

Be a Reading Detective!

Return to

"The Right Dog for the Job"
Student Book pp. 501–511

1 **In which order does Ira learn skills?**

- ☐ disobey, fetch keys, flip light switch
- ☐ fetch keys, disobey, flip light switch
- ☐ fetch keys, flip light switch, disobey
- ☐ flip light switch, disobey, fetch keys

Prove It! What evidence in the selection supports
your answer? Check the boxes. ☑ Make notes.

Evidence	Notes
☐ photographs	
☐ details about the puppy raisers	
☐ details about Sandy's classroom	
☐ details about service-dog training	

Write About It!

SEQUENCE OF EVENTS

Answer question **1** using evidence from the text.

_____

_____

_____

_____

_____

_____

2 **What do the photos and captions tell you about Ira?**

☐ what he learns to do

☐ what he looks like

☐ how he behaves with other dogs

☐ other _____

Prove It! What evidence in the selection supports your answer? Check the boxes. ✔ Make notes.

Evidence	Notes
☐ Ira picks up keys.	
☐ Ira gets off a bus.	
☐ Ira walks in a harness.	
☐	

Write About It!

TEXT AND GRAPHIC FEATURES

Answer question ② using evidence from the text.

_____

_____

_____

_____

_____

_____

_____

boasted
ceased
devised
resourceful
unfortunate

Heroes of Old Tales

1 Old tales often tell about a hero. A hero is usually very **resourceful**. Heroes use quick thinking to get out of danger.

What is another way to say <u>resourceful</u>?

_____

_____

2 Heroes often face enemies. In one story, a hero **devised** a way to keep a monster from turning him into stone. He used a shiny metal shield as a mirror. The monster turned itself into stone!

Have you ever <u>devised</u> a way to solve a problem? How?

_____

_____

_____

3 Sometimes **unfortunate** things happen to a hero. The hero might be hurt or captured. Heroes don't give up, though.

If you met a hero in real life, would that be fortunate or <u>unfortunate</u>? Why?

_____

_____

4 In old stories, heroes often **boasted** about their deeds. They might do this to scare an enemy, or to show that they could be trusted with a big job—such as fighting a monster!

What would you do if someone you knew <u>boasted</u> all the time?

_____

_____

5 A hero often protects a kingdom. Once the danger has **ceased**, the hero might have other adventures.

How do you feel when something scary or annoying has <u>ceased</u>?

_____

_____

THE TRAVELS OF ODYSSEUS

BASED ON GREEK MYTHS

adapted by Judy Rosenbaum

Thousands of years ago, people started telling stories about a huge war. In the stories, Greece fought this war against the city of Troy. After ten years of war, the Greeks won. Then they sailed toward home in their small wooden ships.

Odysseus (oh·DIS·yoos) was an important man in the Greek army. Odysseus and his men faced many strange enemies on their long trip home. Some were giants. Others were beings with great powers. At least one was a god.

Stop **Think** **Write**

STORY STRUCTURE

After the war, what did Odysseus and his men want to do?

_____

_____

_____

Odysseus and his men stopped at an island. They didn't know that a Cyclops (SY·klahps) lived there. A Cyclops is a man-eating giant with one eye. This Cyclops was Polyphemus (pahl·uh·FEE·muhs). Polyphemus trapped the men in a cave. He killed some of them.

Odysseus was very **resourceful**. He spotted a wooden stake. He waited until the Cyclops was asleep and attacked him with the stake. He hurt the giant's one eye.

Stop **Think** **Write**

MAKE INFERENCES

How did Odysseus and his men probably feel in the cave?

_____

_____

_____

Odysseus planned the men's escape carefully. In the morning, Polyphemus let his giant sheep out of the cave. They needed to eat grass in the field. The Cyclops felt the back of each sheep as it left the cave. He checked that the men weren't riding out of the cave on the sheep. But Odysseus had thought of that. He had the men cling to the bellies of the sheep. Polyphemus couldn't tell that the men were getting away.

Stop **Think** **Write**

MAKE INFERENCES

Why did the men do whatever Odysseus told them to do?

Odysseus made one bad mistake. As his ship sailed safely away, he **boasted** loudly about tricking the Cyclops. He called out his own name in his boast. Polyphemus was the son of the sea god, Poseidon (poh·SYD·n). This was **unfortunate** for Odysseus. The sea god vowed that he would make Odysseus suffer. Odysseus would have a long, hard trip home.

Stop | **Think** | **Write**

VOCABULARY

Why was it <u>unfortunate</u> that Poseidon became the enemy of Odysseus?

_____

_____

_____

The island of the Sirens was nearby. These beings had amazing voices. Nobody could resist their songs. Sailors would steer toward the island. Then their ships would crash onto the rocks.

Odysseus **devised** a plan. He gave the men wax earplugs. Odysseus didn't wear earplugs, though. He wanted to hear the Sirens. He had the men tie him up.

The Sirens sang out. The men paid no attention. But the music thrilled Odysseus. Luckily, he was tied up tightly. He wasn't untied until the music **ceased**.

Stop | **Think** | **Write**

What is another way to say <u>ceased</u>?

_____

_____

_____

The ship reached a narrow part of the sea. Steep cliffs were on both sides. Near one cliff was a whirlpool. A sea monster sat across from the whirlpool. This monster had six heads.

Odysseus had to choose. Would he sail closer to the whirlpool or closer to the monster? He decided that the monster could kill only a few men. The whirlpool would suck the ship down and drown everyone. He sailed closer to the monster. Six men died, but the others were safe.

Stop Think Write

CONCLUSIONS

Do you think Odysseus made a wise choice? Why or why not?

_____

_____

_____

Odysseus did make it home to Greece. The sea god Poseidon had his way, though. Odysseus lost all his men in a shipwreck. He was trapped on one island for years. It took him ten long years to reach his home.

A poem called *The Odyssey* tells the story of this trip. The poem was probably made up over 2,500 years ago. Today the word *odyssey* means a long trip with many adventures.

Stop **Think** **Write**

CONCLUSIONS

Why do you think the story of Odysseus has lasted for a long time?

_____

_____

_____

Look Back and Respond

1 What was the main goal of Odysseus and his men after the war ended?

Hint

For a clue, see page 174.

_____

_____

2 What three challenges did Odysseus and his men face on their trip?

Hint

For clues, see pages 175–179.

_____

_____

_____

3 Why did Poseidon want to punish Odysseus?

Hint

For a clue, see page 177.

_____

_____

_____

4 Why was it so dangerous to hear the Sirens' songs?

Hint

For a clue, see page 178.

_____

_____

_____

Be a Reading Detective!

1 **How would you describe Hera?**

☐ motherly ☐ jealous ☐ tired

☐ other _____

Prove It! What evidence in the story supports your answer?
Check the boxes. ☑ Make notes.

Evidence	Notes
☐ She puts serpents in Hercules' cradle.	
☐ She makes Hercules misbehave.	
☐ She thinks of impossible tasks for him.	
☐ text statements about her	

Write About It!

STORY STRUCTURE

Answer question **1** using evidence from the text.

_____

_____

_____

_____

_____

_____

_____

2 **How are Zeus and Hera alike?**

☐ Both are fond of Hercules.

☐ Both are happy.

☐ Both are powerful.

☐ other _____

Prove It! What evidence in the story supports your answer?
Check the boxes. ✔ Make notes.

Evidence	Notes
☐ descriptions of Zeus and Hera	
☐ Hera's actions	
☐ Zeus' actions	
☐	

Write About It!

COMPARE AND CONTRAST

Answer question **2** **using evidence from the text.**

_____

_____

_____

_____

_____

_____

_____

conflicts
dedicate
overcome
publicity
violence

Slavery

1 **Conflicts** can lead to war. Disagreements between the North and the South about slavery led to the Civil War.

What word in this paragraph helps you to understand the meaning of _conflicts_?

_____

2 Cruel treatment and **violence** were common for enslaved people.

What are some bad effects of _violence_? Explain.

_____

_____

_____

3 Some people chose to **dedicate** their time to ending slavery. They risked their lives to help runaways reach freedom.

What do people do when they _dedicate_ themselves to something?

_____

_____

_____

182

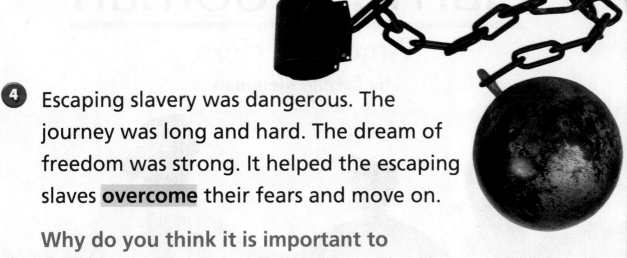

4 Escaping slavery was dangerous. The journey was long and hard. The dream of freedom was strong. It helped the escaping slaves **overcome** their fears and move on.

Why do you think it is important to overcome your fears?

_____

_____

_____

5 Many people in the North spoke out against slavery. They gave speeches. They wrote newspaper articles. This **publicity** helped educate Americans about the cruelty of slavery.

What are two ways to spread information by using publicity?

_____

_____

_____

Harriet Tubman

American Hero
by Estelle Kleinman

Early Life

Harriet Tubman was born in Maryland around 1820. Her parents were enslaved. When she was about five years old, Harriet was put to work. First she worked as a house servant. Later, she worked in the fields.

One day, the man in charge got angry at a field worker. Harriet stepped between the two men. The cruel boss threw a heavy weight. It hit her in the head. Such **violence** against enslaved people was common. The blow caused Harriet problems for the rest of her life.

Stop Think Write

AUTHOR'S PURPOSE

How does the author want you to feel about the boss? How do you know?

_____

_____

_____

A Daring Escape

When Harriet was thirty-two, she received bad news. She was being sold to a new owner. This meant that she would have to leave her family. At that point, Harriet decided to escape.

Harriet met a friendly white woman. The woman hid her in a safe house. Then Harriet was put in a wagon. It took her to another house. Harriet was moved from place to place until she reached freedom in Pennsylvania.

Stop **Think** **Write**

CONCLUSIONS

What made Harriet Tubman want to escape slavery?

_____

_____

_____

The Underground Railroad

Harriet wanted to **dedicate** her life to helping other people escape slavery. She learned that many runaways reached freedom in the same way she did. The trail of safe houses was called the Underground Railroad. It had no tracks or trains. Escaping slaves were called passengers. The person who helped enslaved people reach safety was called the conductor.

Harriet went back for her family. She led her parents north to freedom in Canada.

At the time, they were seventy years old.

Stop **Think** **Write**

CONCLUSIONS

Why do you think that Harriet took the risk of helping enslaved people escape?

_____

_____

_____

A Difficult Trip

Harriet was a very good conductor. Slave hunters put up signs. They were willing to pay $40,000 to anyone who found her. This did not stop the brave conductor.

Harriet made nineteen trips to lead enslaved people to freedom. There were always challenges to **overcome**. Escaping people had to cross swamps, forests, and mountains. They went along back roads at night. Harriet's head wound made her fall asleep suddenly. Her passengers had to wait for her to wake up. Then they would go on their way.

$40,000
REWARD.

Harriet Tubman

RICHARD DORSEY

Stop | Think | Write

VOCABULARY

What are two challenges that Harriet and her passengers had to <u>overcome</u>?

_____

_____

_____

187

A Strong Leader

At times, the escaping slaves would get scared. They were often tired and hungry and cold. Sometimes there were **conflicts** between Harriet and the people she was helping. Some begged to go home. However, Harriet had one rule: there was no going back. If she let some go back, the slave hunters might find the rest. She told her charges that they would be free or die.

Harriet led over 300 enslaved people to freedom. She never lost a passenger!

Stop **Think** **Write**

CONCLUSIONS

Why do you think that Harriet never lost a passenger?

_____

_____

_____

The Civil War

In 1861, the Civil War began. Harriet did her part to help. She served as a nurse for the North. When soldiers were sick, she made a special tea to help cure them.

Harriet also spied for the North. As a conductor, she had gotten to know the land well. She tracked the movement of the Southern troops. She reported what she saw back to the North.

Stop | Think | Write

MAIN IDEA AND DETAILS

In what two ways did Harriet help the North during the Civil War?

_____

_____

_____

Later Life

After the war, Harriet moved to New York. In 1908, she built a home for poor, old people.

Over time, Harriet began to receive publicity for her lifetime spent helping others. Many people learned about the brave woman who had escaped slavery.

In 1913, Harriet Tubman died. She has never been forgotten. In 1944, a ship was named after her. In 1995, a postage stamp came out to honor this great American hero.

Stop Think Write

INFER/PREDICT

What words tell how the author feels about Harriet Tubman?

_____

_____

_____

Look Back and Respond

1 What words would you use to describe Harriet? Explain.

Hint

Think about Harriet's achievements to help you respond.

_____

_____

_____

2 When escaping slaves became scared, how did Harriet persuade them not to turn back?

Hint

For clues, see page 188.

_____

_____

_____

3 Was Harriet's life easier after she escaped from slavery? Explain.

Hint

Clues you can use are on almost every page! See, for example, pages 187, 188, and 189.

_____

_____

_____

Be a Reading Detective!

Return to

"Harvesting Hope"
Student Book pp. 561–571

1 What generalization could you make about migrant farm workers when Chavez was a boy?

☐ They were treated poorly.

☐ They were well organized.

☐ other _____

Prove It! What evidence in the selection supports your answer?
Check the boxes. ☑ Make notes.

Evidence	Notes
☐ illustrations	
☐ what workers thought, said, and did	
☐ details about migrant life	
☐	

Write About It!

CONCLUSIONS AND GENERALIZATIONS

Answer question **1** using evidence from the text.

_____

_____

_____

_____

_____

_____

_____

2 **What is the main idea on pages 566 and 567?**

☐ Chavez stopped harvesting fruit.

☐ Chavez became an organizer.

☐ Chavez was embarrassed at his first meeting.

☐ other _____

Prove It! What evidence in the selection supports your answer? Check the boxes. ✓ Make notes.

Evidence	Notes
☐ illustrations	
☐ details about what Chavez thought and said	
☐ details about what Chavez did	
☐	

Write About It!

Answer question **2** using evidence from the text.

_____

_____

_____

_____

_____

_____

✓ TARGET VOCABULARY

accompany
duty
route
supplies
territory

Exploring the West

1804

Thomas Jefferson sends people to find a way across the United States. He pays for the **1** _____ they need for the trip. He hopes more people will start to move west.

1841

The first wagon train leaves Missouri for California. Forty-seven people bring farm animals to **2** _____ them. They plan to make new homes out west.

1842

More and more families leave their homes in the East. They head to new

3 _____ in the West.

1860

The Pony Express takes mail along

a **4** _____ from Missouri to California. Young boys run the horses fast, so riders get a fresh horse every ten to fifteen miles.

1869

John Powell and his team set out to explore a wild river out west. It is Powell's

5 _____ to ensure his team's safety.

Conquering the Mighty Colorado

by Shirley Granahan

In May of 1869, Major John Wesley Powell and his team of nine men prepared for a trip. They would take four boats and ride down Green River in what is now Wyoming. From there, they would travel down the mighty Colorado River.

The fast-moving water of the Colorado was dangerous. That's why no one had ever made such a trip. Powell knew it would not be easy, but still he planned to go.

Stop · Think · Write

MAIN IDEAS AND DETAILS

Where did Powell and his team plan to go?

_____

_____

_____

A Brave Man

Powell was not afraid. He had faced danger before, and he had lost an arm in the Civil War. Powell was not only a brave soldier, he was also a scientist. His love of science led him to explore the Colorado.

The men pushed their boats from the shore. Powell and his team were on their way. He was glad he had picked men to **accompany** him who were strong and brave. He had a feeling that they would need to be.

Stop   Think   Write

VOCABULARY

Why was it important for Powell to pick strong, brave men to accompany him?

_____

_____

_____

There were almost no towns along the way. The men had **supplies** and stopped to hunt or fish for more food. So far, the trip was not that hard. None of them could imagine what was ahead.

For the first few weeks, the boats were on the Green River, which runs into the Colorado. Each night, Powell made careful notes in his journal. He wrote of the rich, red hills of the **territory** and of the colors of the sunset.

Stop **Think** **Write**

VOCABULARY

What kind of supplies might the men have brought?

_____

_____

_____

Following the River

As they sailed down the river, the look of the land changed. Powell noted sheep high on the steep sides of mountains. He noted lots of elk feeding in open grassland.

Sometimes they had an easy time along the **route** they were taking. Other times, swift waters threatened to tip over the boats. Rocks were also a danger. One day, as they headed down the river, Powell saw a waterfall ahead. "Look out!" he shouted.

Stop · Think · Write

MAIN IDEAS AND DETAILS

Tell one way the land changed as the men moved along the river.

_____

_____

_____

It was too late. One of the boats went over the falls and smashed into the rocks. Men and supplies from the boat fell into the water. The river carried most of their supplies away. Two men began to swim to a small island. Another man held on to a rock in the river.

Powell's team saved the man on the rock. Then they saved the men from the island.

The next day, one of the men told Powell he was leaving. The rest of the men climbed into the three boats they had left and kept going. They would not give up. They felt it was their **duty** to go on.

Stop Think Write

INFER AND PREDICT

Why did one of the men leave the team?

_____

_____

_____

Carry On!

Soon they reached the place where the Green River joins the Colorado River. They stopped to repair their boats and rest. Then they set off down the Colorado.

The men hit more rapids than they had expected. Fast-moving water rocked the tiny boats. At times, the water was too rough, and the men walked on shore. They used ropes to pull the boats through the water. At other times, they had to carry the boats over land.

Stop **Think** **Write**

MAIN IDEAS AND DETAILS

Why didn't the men ride in the boats all the way down the river?

_____

_____

_____

A Job Well Done

Three more men had had enough. They thought it was too dangerous to continue, so they left the team. There were only six men left.

Only two days later, the six men had traveled through the Grand Canyon and completed their journey. They had traveled more than a thousand miles in less than a hundred days.

Powell's trip helped Americans learn about lands in the West. Soon, families came to build homes along the mighty Colorado.

Stop **Think** **Write**

MAIN IDEAS AND DETAILS

How did Powell's trip help other Americans?

_____

_____

_____

Look Back and Respond

1 **Why did Powell explore the Colorado?**

Hint

For a clue, see page 195.

_____

_____

_____

2 **Why had no one ever gone down the Colorado before?**

Hint

For a clue, see page 194.

_____

_____

_____

3 **Was Powell's team brave? Explain.**

Hint

Reread to look for clues on different pages.

_____

_____

_____

4 **Do you think the men who left early regretted their decisions? Explain.**

Hint

Think about how Powell and the men who reached the destination must have felt.

_____

_____

_____

Be a Reading Detective!

Return to

"Sacagawea"
Student Book pp. 589–603

① **Which details support the idea that Sacagawea was important to the expedition?**

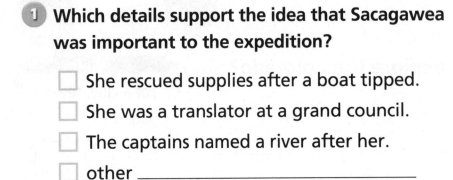

- ☐ She rescued supplies after a boat tipped.
- ☐ She was a translator at a grand council.
- ☐ The captains named a river after her.
- ☐ other _____

Prove It! What evidence in the selection supports your answer?
Check the boxes. ✓ Make notes.

Evidence	Notes
☐ illustrations	
☐ what Sacagawea said and did	
☐ what the captains did	
☐	

Write About It!

MAIN IDEAS AND DETAILS

Answer question ① using evidence from the text.

_____

_____

_____

_____

_____

_____

2 **What conclusion could you draw about Sacagawea?**

☐ She was brave.

☐ She cared only for her son.

☐ She was afraid of new things.

☐ other _____

Prove It! What evidence in the selection supports your answer? Check the boxes. ✓ Make notes.

Evidence	Notes
☐ how she acted in a crisis	
☐ how she made sure to see the ocean	
☐ how she didn't let the captain take her son	
☐	

Write About It!

CONCLUSIONS AND GENERALIZATIONS

Answer question **2** using evidence from the text.

_____

_____

_____

_____

_____

_____

_____

201B

✓ TARGET VOCABULARY

appreciate
feats
introduce
promptly
suggest

Robots

Check the answer.

1 We _____ robots because they help us. They do many tasks that make life easier.

☐ **apologize** ☐ **appreciate** ☐ **recall**

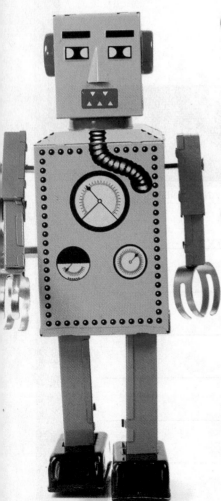

2 Robots can perform many _____. Robots can put together parts on an assembly line. Other robots work in space.

☐ **feats** ☐ **organisms** ☐ **obstacles**

3 When robots work, they don't waste time. They can do a job _____ and well.

☐ **directly** ☐ **regretfully** ☐ **promptly**

4 Some robots look like humans. They can walk and speak. They can even _____ themselves to people.

☐ **introduce**　☐ **accompany**　☐ **suggest**

5 A man was writing a story about imitation people. He did not know what to call them. He asked his brother to _____ a name. Can you guess the word the brother made up? Robot!

☐ **assist**　☐ **rescue**　☐ **suggest**

6 Tell about a time when you got a gift that you could <u>appreciate</u>.

_____

_____

_____

7 What do you say when you <u>introduce</u> yourself?

_____

_____

_____

Thought for the Day

by Carol Alexander

It was Brian's birthday. Aunt Pam and Uncle Sid gave him a special gift. It was a robot. Brian had other robots at home, but this one was different.

"This robot can think for you," Uncle Sid explained. "You'll never have to think for yourself again."

"Great!" said Brian. "How does it perform these **feats**?"

Aunt Pam told him, "We fed the robot all kinds of facts. It knows your favorite foods. It knows the games and books you like."

Stop | Think | Write

VOCABULARY

What kinds of feats might a thinking robot perform?

_____

_____

_____

Brian turned to the robot. "What should I name you?" he asked his new friend.

"TIR is a good name," the robot said. Its lights flashed. "That stands for The Idea Robot. I will give you good ideas."

"He sure is smart! Thanks, Uncle Sid and Aunt Pam. I really **appreciate** this gift." Brian felt very lucky. Now he would not have to think anymore. His thinking would be done for him.

That afternoon, Brian called his friend Gail. "Come on over. I want to **introduce** you to a new friend."

Stop Think Write

What did Brian most appreciate about his present?

_____

_____

_____

Gail arrived shortly. "Meet TIR," Brian said to her. "He's my new robot. Watch what he can do." Brian turned to TIR. "I'm thirsty. What should I drink?"

"Drink a glass of orange juice, drink a glass of juice," the robot answered.

Gail's eyes grew wide. "Wow! He really is smart!"

Brian had another question. "I have to go to a birthday party on Saturday. I don't know what to wear. What do you **suggest**?"

"Wear your bright blue shirt! Blue shirt!" the robot replied quickly.

Stop | Think | Write

CAUSE AND EFFECT

What makes Gail and Brian think the robot is smart?

_____

_____

_____

All day, Brian asked TIR questions. TIR answered each one **promptly**. For instance, Brian asked, "What game should I play?"

TIR answered, "Play a game of checkers. I will play against you."

"That's amazing!" Gail said. "Your robot can play checkers. Do you think he will tell you how to beat him?"

"Let's see," Brian said.

First, the robot placed the checkers on the board. He did not make a single mistake. He beeped to show he was ready to play.

Stop | Think | Write

THEME

Do you think it would be fun to play with someone who never makes a mistake? Why?

_____

_____

_____

"Which color should I be?" Brian asked.

"You should be red. I'll be black." They started to play. TIR was very helpful. He pointed to a red checker. "Move this one here." Brian did as he was told.

TIR told Brian how to make each move, so Brian won the game. The robot didn't seem to mind losing.

"That's great," Gail said. "You can win without even trying."

"I know," Brian sighed. "That's the problem. This is boring. Let's go out and play, Gail."

Stop **Think** **Write**

THEME

Why does Brian think the game of checkers is boring?

_____

_____

_____

TIR's lights flashed and blinked. "Ride your bike in the park. Ride your bike in the park."

"I don't want to ride my bike right now!" Brian yelled. "Gail, I can't stand this robot anymore!"

Brian threw a towel over TIR's head. The robot began to beep, squeak, and clatter. Gail looked worried. "He won't hurt us, will he?"

"Drink a bright blue shirt. Wear a glass of orange juice. Read a bike. Ride a book. I am TIR, the checker in the park, the park, the park," TIR said.

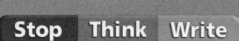

Stop | Think | Write

CAUSE AND EFFECT

What makes the robot act strangely?

_____

_____

_____

"Let's take out his battery," Gail said.

"Yes!" Brian agreed. He opened up the robot and removed the battery. That did it. The robot was finally quiet.

"That's much better," Gail pointed out.

"You can say that again!" Brian laughed. He looked at the robot, then shook his head. "I learned a good lesson. Sometimes it's better to think for yourself."

"That's the thought for the day," Gail replied. "Come on, let's go out and play ball."

Stop | Think | Write

What does Gail think about the robot?

_____

_____

_____

Look Back and Respond

1 Why does Brian like the robot at first?

_____

_____

_____

Hint

For clues, see pages 204, 205, and 206.

2 Who is a better friend, Gail or the robot? Explain.

_____

_____

_____

Hint

For clues, see pages 208, 209, and 210.

3 What does Brian learn in the story?

_____

_____

_____

Hint

For clues, see pages 209 and 210.

4 Do you think Brian will turn on TIR again? Explain.

_____

_____

_____

Hint

Think about what happened in the story. Think about what you would do.

Be a Reading Detective!

1 **What is the theme of the story?**

☐ Hamsters improve people's lives.

☐ People like doing things together.

☐ Living without TV is more fun than living with it.

Prove It! What evidence in the story supports your answer?
Check the boxes. ✓ Make notes.

Evidence	Notes
☐ what happens while the TV is on	
☐ what happens while the TV is off	
☐ the illustrations on pages 628 and 633	

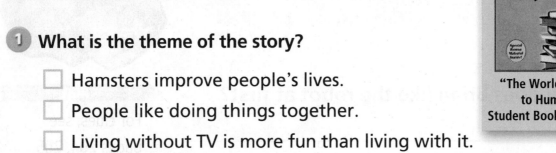

Write About It!

THEME

Answer question **1** using evidence from the text.

_____

_____

_____

_____

_____

_____

"The World According to Humphrey"
Student Book pp. 625–637

Return to

211A

2 **Which adjective best describes Humphrey?**

☐ bored   ☐ easygoing

☐ resourceful   ☐ funny

Prove It! What evidence in the story supports your answer?
Check the boxes. ☑ Make notes.

Evidence	Notes
☐ how Humphrey gets out of his cage	
☐ how Humphrey unplugs the TV	
☐	

Write About It!

UNDERSTANDING CHARACTERS

Answer question **2** using evidence from the text.

_____

_____

_____

_____

_____

_____

_____

211B

✓ TARGET VOCABULARY

approve
candidates
denied
intelligent
politics

How to Change Laws

If people are ① _____ their rights, they ask for a change in the laws. A new law must be fair to all people.

People can write letters. They can call lawmakers to ask for changes. The lawmakers work with others. Together they make ② _____ choices about how to change the laws.

If the lawmakers do
not agree, they suggest
more changes. If enough of
them **3** _____,
the law is changed.

Many people decide to work
in **4** _____ to pass fair laws.
People in Congress pass laws for the whole
country. We also elect local people to pass laws
for our state or city.

People who want to be elected give
speeches. They explain their ideas. Voters ask
questions of the **5** _____.
Then voters elect the person they think will do
the best job.

Getting the Vote

by Shirley Granahan

What do you think of when you hear the name Susan B. Anthony? Some people think of the first woman pictured on U.S. money. Other people think of a woman who tried to make sure women were not **denied** equal rights.

Stop **Think** **Write**

INFER AND PREDICT

What do you predict this selection will tell you about Susan B. Anthony?

_____

_____

_____

Susan B. Anthony was born in 1820. A woman's life then was not like it is today. Some people did not think girls were as **intelligent** as boys. Girls were not pushed to learn or speak up in school.

Women did not work outside the home. They were supposed to marry and have children. Women were supposed to take care of their homes and families.

Stop | **Think** | **Write**

VOCABULARY

Write another word that means the same as <u>intelligent</u>.

_____

Susan B. Anthony's father was different. He wanted all his children to be treated the same. Susan had the same schooling, chores, and rights as her brothers.

One teacher thought only boys needed to know math. She would not teach Susan long division. Susan's father took her out of that school!

Stop **Think** **Write**

How did Susan's father show that he believed men and women should be treated the same way?

_____

_____

_____

Susan wanted all women to have the same rights as men. She told her ideas to others. Her speeches made some men angry.

These men did not want women to have the same rights they had. They thought that **politics**, or how a government is run, was just for men. They did not **approve** of women talking about such things!

Stop   Think   Write

VOCABULARY

Why do you think some men did not approve of Susan giving speeches?

_____

_____

_____

Then Susan met Elizabeth Cady Stanton. Elizabeth had the same strong ideas about rights for women.

Women could not vote for a U.S. President at that time. Susan and Elizabeth wanted women to be able to vote. Elizabeth wrote speeches. Susan gave them. Some men were very unhappy with Susan and Elizabeth. That did not stop the two women.

Stop **Think** **Write**

CAUSE AND EFFECT

Why did Susan and Elizabeth make a good team?

_____

_____

_____

A President was to be elected in 1872. Susan read all about the **candidates**. She wanted to vote for the best person for the job. So she went to the voting place.

People there said she could not vote. They would not let her in. Susan did get in. She voted. Some men became very angry. They had Susan arrested. They said it was a crime for a woman to vote.

Stop **Think** **Write**

SEQUENCE OF EVENTS

What happened after Susan voted?

_____

_____

_____

That did not stop Susan. In fact, she and Elizabeth thought it could help their plans. They had marches and meetings all across the United States.

As years passed, Susan became ill. She could not give speeches. Other women continued the fight, and in 1920, the Nineteenth Amendment was passed. It gave women the right to vote. Today, women not only vote, they get elected!

Stop   Think   Write

CAUSE AND EFFECT

What happened when Susan became ill?

_____

_____

_____

Look Back and Respond

1 **How is a woman's life today different from a woman's life in the 1800s?**

Hint

For a clue, see page 215.

_____

_____

_____

2 **How did Susan help to change the laws about voting?**

Hint

For clues, see each page from 217 on.

_____

_____

_____

3 **What effect did being arrested have on Susan?**

Hint

For a clue, see page 220.

_____

_____

_____

4 **Why do people want to vote?**

Hint

Think about having a say in what happens.

_____

_____

_____

Be a Reading Detective!

"I Could Do That!"
Student Book pp. 655–665

Return to

1 **Why did Esther Morris move to Illinois?**

- ☐ to marry John Morris
- ☐ to be on the frontier
- ☐ to claim her dead husband's land

Prove It! What evidence in the selection supports your answer?
Check the boxes. ☑ Make notes.

Evidence	Notes
☐ what Esther says after Artemus dies	
☐ details in the text after Artemus's death	
☐	

Write About It!

CAUSE AND EFFECT

Answer question **1** using evidence from the text.

_____

_____

_____

_____

_____

_____

_____

2 **Why did the author tell Esther Morris's story?**

☐ to tell the story of women's rights

☐ to tell how one person can make a difference

☐ to tell about life in the 1800s

Prove It! What evidence in the selection supports your answer?
Check the boxes. ☑ Make notes.

Evidence	Notes
☐ details about Esther's successes	
☐ beliefs about women in the 1800s	
☐ the illustrations of Esther doing things	

Write About It!

Answer question 2 using evidence from the text.

_____

_____

_____

_____

_____

_____

_____

continent
dense
moisture
resources
shallow

Redwood Trees

1 Redwood trees grow in North America. They are the tallest trees on the **continent**.

North America is one <u>continent</u>. Name another continent.

_____

2 Redwood trees require plenty of **moisture**. They grow in places where winters are rainy and summers are foggy.

What provides <u>moisture</u> for trees and other plants?

_____

_____

_____

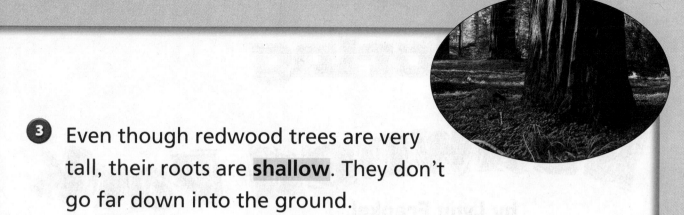

3 Even though redwood trees are very tall, their roots are **shallow**. They don't go far down into the ground.

Write a word that means the opposite of <u>shallow</u>.

_____

4 Redwood trees are important natural **resources**. People use the trees for wood.

What are some other natural <u>resources</u> that people use?

_____

_____

_____

5 Fallen needles from redwood trees form a **dense** mat on the ground. The needles make it hard for other trees to grow.

Would you prefer to live in a <u>dense</u> city or in a small town? Explain.

_____

_____

_____

Exploring Redwood Park

by Lynn Frankel

Mrs. Keith and her students are exploring Redwood National Park in California. The park was founded in 1968 to protect the redwood trees and other **resources** in the region.

Redwood National Park

California

Pacific Ocean

Stop Think Write

TEXT AND GRAPHIC FEATURES

Where is Redwood National Park?

_____

_____

_____

An American Indian greeted the visitors. "Welcome to Redwood National Park!" he said. "My name is Standing Elk. I will show you the park today."

Standing Elk stepped onto the trail. Paco, Sarah, Carlos, Lakota, and Mrs. Keith followed him.

"Our park has many kinds of trees," Standing Elk said. "However, it's named for an exceptional tree, the redwood. Redwoods are the tallest trees on the **continent**. Actually, they're the tallest trees in the world!"

Stop | **Think** | **Write**

MAIN IDEAS AND DETAILS

What is special about redwood trees?

_____

_____

_____

"Wow!" said Paco. He stared up at the redwoods. "I can't see the tops of the trees."

"That's because the trees are so tall," Standing Elk said. "It's also because the forest is so **dense**. These trees grow close together."

"Look how big!" The four students tried to touch hands around a redwood's trunk. They couldn't reach!

"Some of the trees in the park have been growing for six hundred years," Standing Elk said. "Some redwoods live for two thousand years!"

Stop | **Think** | **Write**

VOCABULARY

Why is the redwood forest <u>dense</u>?

_____

_____

_____

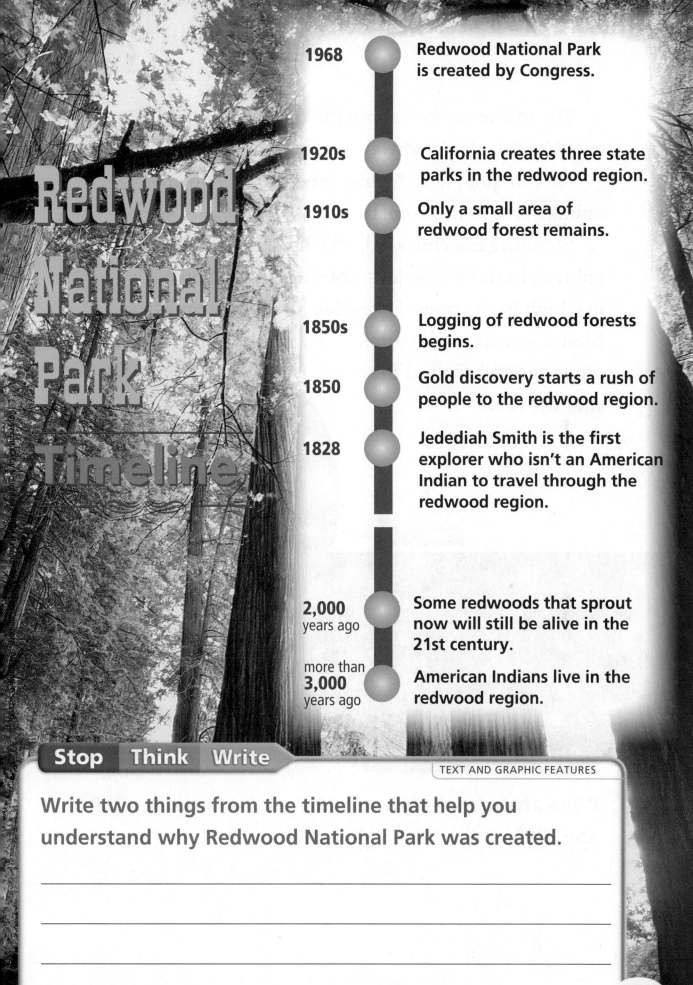

Redwood National Park Timeline

1968	Redwood National Park is created by Congress.
1920s	California creates three state parks in the redwood region.
1910s	Only a small area of redwood forest remains.
1850s	Logging of redwood forests begins.
1850	Gold discovery starts a rush of people to the redwood region.
1828	Jedediah Smith is the first explorer who isn't an American Indian to travel through the redwood region.
2,000 years ago	Some redwoods that sprout now will still be alive in the 21st century.
more than **3,000** years ago	American Indians live in the redwood region.

Stop Think Write

TEXT AND GRAPHIC FEATURES

Write two things from the timeline that help you understand why Redwood National Park was created.

_____

_____

_____

227

The group walked along the trail. They were awed by the giant redwoods.

"It's so quiet here," whispered Sarah. "Do any animals live in this forest?"

Standing Elk chuckled. "We have many animals here. Wrens, jays, chickadees, and owls live high in the trees. Foxes live in hollow trunks. Moles, insects, and worms dig in the soil around the **shallow** roots."

Stellar's jay

Stop Think Write

What animals are shown in the photos on pages 228 and 229?

_____

_____

_____

northern spotted owl

Suddenly a leaf jumped next to Carlos. "That leaf looks like a frog!" he said.

"Good eye, Carlos!" Standing Elk pointed to the small frog. "Just like redwoods, these frogs need lots of **moisture**. They like the rainy, mild climate of this forest habitat."

"Are any of the animals dangerous?" asked Mrs. Keith. She looked around nervously.

"Just about any animal can be dangerous. It's best to keep your distance," Standing Elk warned. "No one wants to mess with a black bear or a bobcat."

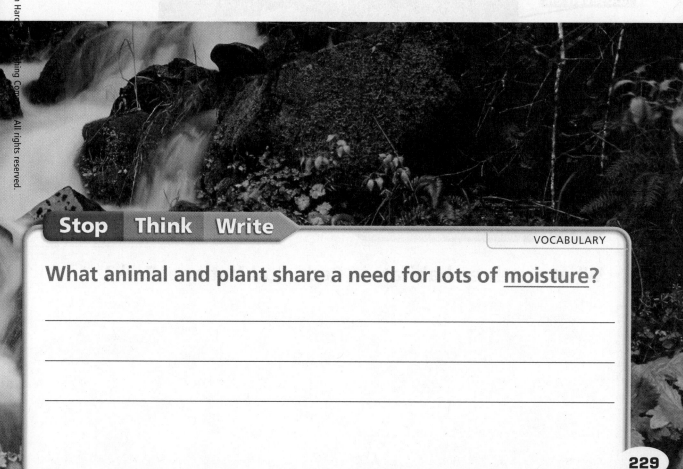

Stop | **Think** | **Write**

What animal and plant share a need for lots of <u>moisture</u>?

_____

_____

_____

"Large animals live in other areas of the park, too," said Standing Elk. "Elk live in the grasslands of our prairies. Whales, sea lions, and dolphins live in the ocean along the coast of the park."

bald eagle

"I thought this park was just about redwood trees," Lakota said. "I can see that it's not."

Standing Elk smiled. "There is a lot to see, and plenty of time to see it. The park isn't going anywhere."

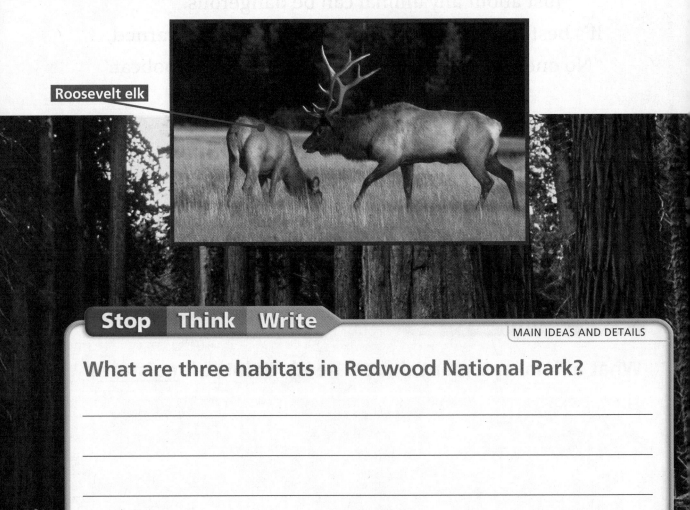

Roosevelt elk

Stop | Think | Write

MAIN IDEAS AND DETAILS

What are three habitats in Redwood National Park?

_____

_____

_____

Look Back and Respond

1 What is the purpose of Redwood National Park?

Hint

For a clue, see page 224.

_____

_____

_____

2 Look at the map on page 224. How does it help you understand the location of Redwood National Park?

Hint

Think about what you see when you look at the map.

_____

_____

_____

3 How do different animals live in and use redwood trees?

Hint

For clues, see pages 228 and 229.

_____

_____

_____

Be a Reading Detective!

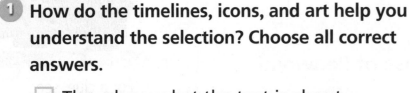

Return to

"The Ever-Living Tree"
Student Book pp. 685–699

① How do the timelines, icons, and art help you understand the selection? Choose all correct answers.

☐ They show what the text is about.

☐ They show when something happened.

☐ They make the selection more fun to read.

Prove It! What evidence in the selection supports your answer?

Check the boxes. ✓ Make notes.

Evidence	Notes
☐ timelines show years for events	
☐ icons identify timeline events	
☐ icons give clues to the text	
☐ art at bottom of page illustrates text	

Write About It!

TEXT AND GRAPHIC FEATURES

Answer question ① using evidence from the text.

_____

_____

_____

_____

_____

_____

_____

2 **Which of these events took place most recently?**

☐ The kingdom of Kanem was a trading center.

☐ Marco Polo's father died.

☐ The Great Wall of China was built.

Prove It! What evidence in the selection supports your answer?
Check the boxes. ☑ Make notes.

Evidence	Notes
☐ details about Kanem	
☐ details about Marco Polo	
☐ details about Chinese history	

Write About It!

SEQUENCE OF EVENTS

Answer question 2 using evidence from the text.

_____

_____

_____

_____

_____

_____

affection
bond
companion
inseparable
suffered

Animal Friends

A dog can be a great **companion**. Most dogs are friendly, and they will go wherever you take them. Dogs can keep people from feeling lonely.

You can adopt a dog from an animal shelter. Some dogs have **suffered** cruelty from other owners. These dogs can be scared of people. It will take extra time and attention to gain their trust.

Most dogs will show you **affection** if you take good care of them. They will lick you or cuddle with you. You can show your dog affection by brushing, petting, or cuddling it.

People usually have a strong **bond** with their dogs. Dogs can sense when their owners are sick or sad. People know when their dogs need extra care, too.

Some people and their dogs are **inseparable**. They go everywhere together.

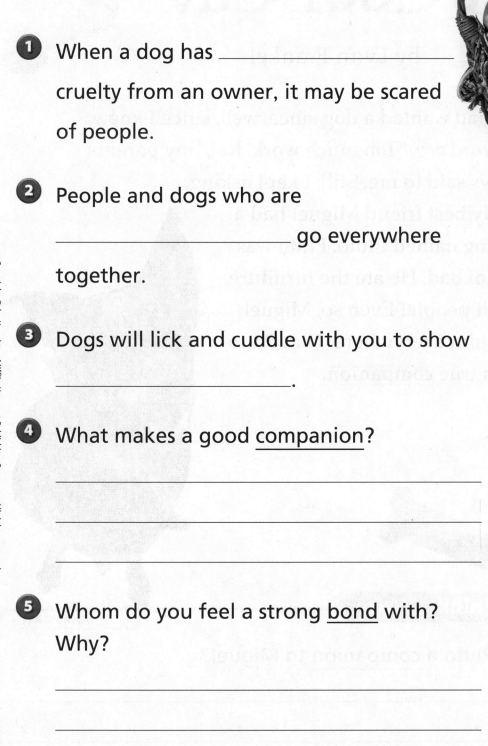

1 When a dog has _____ cruelty from an owner, it may be scared of people.

2 People and dogs who are _____ go everywhere together.

3 Dogs will lick and cuddle with you to show _____.

4 What makes a good <u>companion</u>?

_____

_____

_____

5 Whom do you feel a strong <u>bond</u> with? Why?

_____

_____

_____

A Cool Cat

by Lynn Frankel

I had wanted a dog since, well, since I knew the word *dog*. "Too much work, Kai," my parents always said to me. Still, I kept asking.

My best friend Miguel had a big dog named Pluto. Pluto was kind of bad. He ate the furniture. He bit people! Even so, Miguel took him everywhere. That Pluto was a true **companion**.

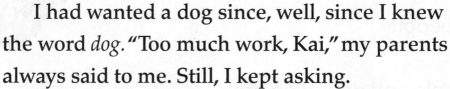

Stop   Think   Write

VOCABULARY

How was Pluto a **companion** to Miguel?

_____

_____

_____

234

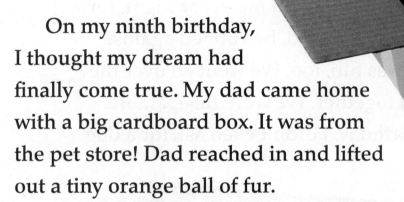

On my ninth birthday,
I thought my dream had
finally come true. My dad came home
with a big cardboard box. It was from
the pet store! Dad reached in and lifted
out a tiny orange ball of fur.

"Meow," it said.

I tried to hide my disappointment. A cat?
What good is a cat? The furry thing looked
up at me. What could I do?
I named him Toby.

Stop | Think | Write

INFER AND PREDICT

Why do you think Kai's parents gave him a cat instead of a dog?

_____

_____

_____

Toby didn't walk me to school like Miguel's dog did. He wouldn't fetch a stick either.

"Well, what does he do?" Miguel asked.

He slept on my bed with me every night, for one thing. When I was sad, he rubbed against my face. Toby was fun, too. We went all over the neighborhood together. We were **inseparable**. On my next birthday, I didn't even ask for a dog.

Stop Think Write

COMPARE AND CONTRAST

How did Kai change between his ninth and tenth birthdays?

_____

_____

_____

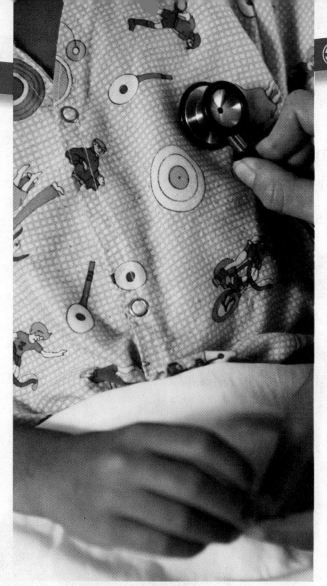

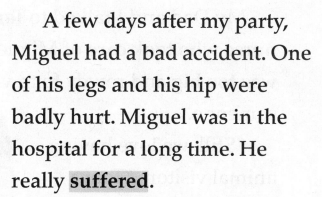

A few days after my party, Miguel had a bad accident. One of his legs and his hip were badly hurt. Miguel was in the hospital for a long time. He really **suffered**.

When I went to see him, Miguel seemed sad. He said he hated being in bed all the time. I think he was scared, too. He wouldn't say so.

Miguel did keep saying how much he missed Pluto. That's when I first got the idea.

Stop | Think | Write

INFER AND PREDICT

What idea do you think Kai has?

_____

_____

_____

My Dad and I talked to Tanya. She was the nurse who took care of Miguel. Tanya said Pluto was too big and rowdy for a visit. He might hurt someone.

"Still, we love having animal visitors," Tanya explained. "They can help sick people get well faster. Just petting an animal can make people feel less worried or less lonely." I knew that was true.

"Hey! What about Toby?" I asked. We all agreed that Toby would be a good visitor.

Stop **Think** **Write**

COMPARE AND CONTRAST

Why is Toby a better hospital visitor than Pluto?

_____

_____

_____

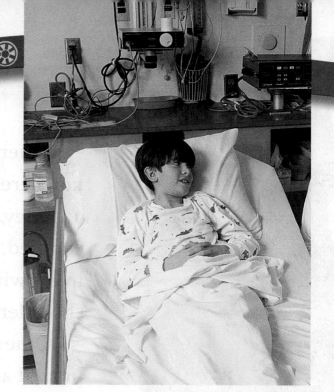

The next day, Dad and I took Toby to visit Miguel. He was lying in bed just staring at the wall. Before I could even say "Hi" to Miguel, Toby had jumped onto his bed.

"What?" Miguel started. "Your cat? I don't even like cats."

I decided to give Miguel some time alone with Toby. Maybe he would change his mind. Maybe they would form a **bond**.

Stop | Think | Write

UNDERSTANDING CHARACTERS

How is Miguel feeling when Kai arrives? Explain.

_____

_____

_____

When I came back, Miguel was nowhere in sight. Neither was Toby.

"Hey, we're over here!" Miguel shouted. He was speeding down the hall in his wheelchair. Toby was riding on his shoulder!

Other kids gathered around. Toby purred and nuzzled Miguel's neck. "He's pretty cool, for a cat," he said, giving Toby one last belly rub.

"You see," Tanya said. "Sometimes **affection** is the best medicine."

Stop | Think | Write

VOCABULARY

How does Miguel show <u>affection</u> for Toby?

_____

_____

_____

Look Back and Respond

1 **How is Toby a good companion?**

_____

_____

_____

Hint

Clues you can use are on almost every page!

2 **How are Toby and Pluto alike? How are they different?**

_____

_____

_____

Hint

For clues, see pages 234 and 236.

3 **How does Toby's visit affect Miguel?**

_____

_____

_____

Hint

For clues, see pages 237, 239, and 240.

4 **Do you think animals can help sick or sad people feel better? Explain.**

_____

_____

_____

Hint

Your answers to questions 1 and 3 might help you.

Be a Reading Detective!

Return to

"Owen and Mzee"
Student Book pp. 717–727

1 **How are Owen and Mzee different?**

☐ One is a baby; the other is 130 years old.

☐ Owen likes water; so does Mzee.

☐ Owen nuzzles Mzee; Mzee stretches out his neck.

Prove It! What evidence in the selection supports your answer?
Check the boxes. ✓ Make notes.

Evidence	Notes
☐ descriptions of Owen	
☐ descriptions of Mzee	
☐ photographs	

Write About It!

COMPARE AND CONTRAST

Answer question **1** using evidence from the text.

_____

_____

_____

_____

_____

_____

_____

2 **In what ways did Mzee look after Owen?**

☐ He was a safe companion for Owen.

☐ He made Owen feel more comfortable in the park.

☐ other _____

Prove It! What evidence in the selection supports your answer?
Check the boxes. ☑ Make notes.

Evidence	Notes
☐ how Mzee acts with Owen	
☐ how Owen acts in the park	
☐	

Write About It!

MAIN IDEAS AND DETAILS

Answer question 2 using evidence from the text.

_____

_____

_____

_____

_____

_____

_____

241B

average
calculated
centuries
inspector
progress

The Future

1 No one knows for sure what the future will be like. Still, most people think that there will be a lot of **progress** made in science.

How does practicing something help you make progress?

_____

_____

_____

2 In the past two **centuries**, people invented bicycles and computers. In the next two centuries, people might invent rocket shoes or a way to talk to animals.

Write these units of time in order from least to greatest: 2 years, 2 minutes, 2 centuries, 2 weeks.

_____

_____

_____

3 Today's scientists have **calculated** that it would take about ten years to reach Pluto. In the future, we might be able to get there quicker.

If you <u>calculated</u> the months until your birthday, what would you do first?

_____

_____

_____

4 In the future, a robot **inspector**, instead of a mechanic, might check cars.

If you were your school's safety <u>inspector</u>, what would your job be?

_____

_____

_____

5 In the future, the **average** family might drive a flying vehicle.

Write a synonym for <u>average</u>.

_____

The Kirks

by Lynn Frankel

Meet the Kirks, an **average** family living in the year 3010. Mrs. Kirk is a rocket pilot. Every day she flies people around the Milky Way Galaxy. Mr. Kirk is a rocket **inspector**. He makes sure all the rockets fly safely. Daughter Janey is in the fourth grade. She's the captain of the Sunbeams, her school's volleyball team. Janey's older brother, Tom, is in the eighth grade. He's a talented artist.

Stop Think Write

STORY STRUCTURE

When does this story take place?

_____

_____

_____

244

Life for the Kirks is very different from what you and I know today. The Kirks live in a space station instead of a house. They fly rockets to school and work. A robot does all their cleaning!

Yes, a lot of **progress** has been made in 1,000 years. Still, some things never change. The Kirks are very busy. Family life still takes a lot of effort.

Stop Think Write

VOCABULARY

What progress has been made in 1,000 years?

_____

_____

_____

Janey Kirk is very excited today. The Sunbeams are playing an important game.

"Are you coming to the game?" she asks Tom as he rushes to the door.

"I can't! I'm already late for a painting class!"

"Wait! Don't forget this!" Mrs. Kirk stops Tom at the door and hands him a muffin. "Nobody leaves home without breakfast."

Stop | **Think** | **Write**

Why is Janey excited today?

_____

_____

_____

Janey waves goodbye to Tom. She asks her mother, "Mom, you and Dad are coming, aren't you?"

"I'm going to try, but I have to fly to Zygon today. I might not get back in time."

Mr. Kirk enters the room and fixes his tie. "Do you think I should wear this blue tie or my red one?"

"Red, Dad. Red is much better with that shirt. Are you coming to the game tonight?"

"I've **calculated** the timing over and over. There's no way I can inspect the new rocket *and* see the game. Sorry, Janey."

Stop Think Write

STORY STRUCTURE

Why can't Mr. and Mrs. Kirk go to Janey's game?

_____

_____

_____

Janey tries not to show it, but her feelings are hurt. The other Sunbeams can see something is wrong. In the first play of the game, Janey misses an easy serve.

"Come on, Janey!" the coach yells. "Wake up out there! Check your shoes!"

Janey checks her volleyball shoes. All of the players are wearing the same special shoes that let them jump incredibly high. It makes for an exciting game.

Stop **Think** **Write**

AUTHOR'S PURPOSE

What is the author's purpose in describing the shoes that volleyball players wear in 3010?

_____

_____

_____

There are only 30 seconds left to play. The ball is hit very high. It nearly touches the gym ceiling.

"I've got it!" Janey jumps. A flash of red catches her eye. It's her father's tie! She sees her whole family in the stands!

"Go, Janey!" they all yell.

Janey is so happy that she spikes the ball over the net. Score! The Sunbeams win!

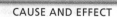

Stop **Think** **Write**

CAUSE AND EFFECT

How does seeing her family affect Janey?

_____

_____

_____

The family rushes to congratulate Janey.

"What happened?" she asks. "I thought you couldn't come."

"I cancelled my class," Tom explains. "And Mom and Dad agreed to work this weekend instead."

Mr. and Mrs. Kirk hug Janey. "We wouldn't miss this!"

Whether it's the year 2010 or 3010, families have a lot in common. **Centuries** may pass, but busy families find time to be together.

Stop Think Write

How many <u>centuries</u> pass between the years 2010 and 3010?

_____

_____

_____

Look Back and Respond

1 **Who are the main characters? Explain.**

_____

_____

_____

Hint

Clues you can use are on almost every page!

2 **In this story, what things in the future are different than they are today?**

_____

_____

_____

Hint

For clues, see pages 244, 245, and 248.

3 **Why do you think Janey's brother and parents make the effort to see her game?**

_____

_____

_____

Hint

For a clue, see page 250.

4 **What do you think is the author's main purpose for this story? Explain.**

_____

_____

_____

Hint

Study the illustrations for clues.

Be a Reading Detective!

Return to

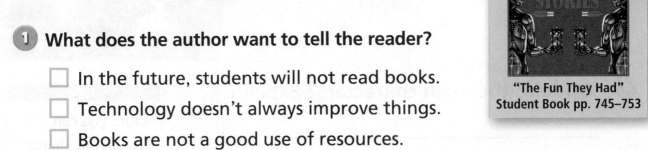

"The Fun They Had"
Student Book pp. 745–753

1 **What does the author want to tell the reader?**

☐ In the future, students will not read books.

☐ Technology doesn't always improve things.

☐ Books are not a good use of resources.

Prove It! What evidence in the story supports your answer?
Check the boxes. ☑ Make notes.

Evidence	Notes
☐ how Margie and Tommy learn	
☐ what Tommy says about old schools	
☐ Margie's thoughts about old schools	

Write About It!

AUTHOR'S PURPOSE

Answer question **1** using evidence from the text.

_____

_____

_____

_____

_____

_____

_____

2 **How does Tommy behave with Margie?**

☐ He acts as if he is smarter because he is older.

☐ He will not tell her what he has discovered.

☐ other _____

Prove It! What evidence in the story supports
your answer? Check the boxes. ☑ Make notes.

Evidence	Notes
☐ what Tommy says and does	
☐ how Margie responds to Tommy	
☐	

Write About It!

UNDERSTANDING CHARACTERS

Answer question 2 using evidence from the text.

_____

_____

_____

_____

_____

_____

_____

✓ TARGET VOCABULARY

assist
favor
intends
nourishing
peculiar

1 Spiders **assist** gardeners without knowing it. Spiders eat up bugs that can harm plants. That is a big help. Gardeners like spiders!

How do you <u>assist</u> people at home? Explain.

_____

_____

_____

2 Bats eat the mosquitoes that bite us. We can return this **favor** by leaving bats alone. They are part of our outdoor world.

What is the last <u>favor</u> you asked a friend to do for you?

_____

_____

_____

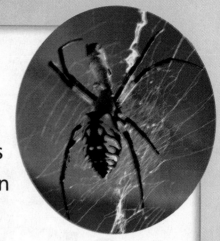

3 A gardener often **intends** to attract bees to his garden. Bees pollinate plants when they flit from flower to flower.

Tell what a gardener intends to do when he puts up a scarecrow.

_____

_____

_____

4 Tiny ants don't need much food to live on. Even a crumb from your sandwich can be a **nourishing** snack for the bug.

What is a nourishing snack for a bird?

_____

_____

_____

5 The black swallowtail butterfly has a **peculiar** meal plan. It only likes to eat carrot plants.

What is another word that has the same meaning as peculiar?

_____

Coming Home

by Carol Alexander

"Class," said Mrs. Woods, "do me a **favor**. Show Maria around."

Maria was starting her school year a little late. She had just moved to this town. She liked her new classroom. Maria pointed to a glass tank. "What are those?" she asked. "They look funny."

"They're monarch butterflies," said Paul.

"They don't *look* like butterflies," Maria replied.

Stop Think Write

STORY STRUCTURE

Where does the story take place?

_____

_____

_____

Hector said, "Right now, they're caterpillars. But soon they will turn into butterflies."

The caterpillars had bright stripes. They were yellow, black, and white. Maria watched the bugs eat leaves. "Do they eat grass, too?"

"No," Carmen answered. "They only eat milkweed leaves."

"Well, they really are **peculiar**," Maria said.

"They really like those leaves," Paul told her. "They must taste good."

"How do they turn into butterflies?" asked Maria.

"Look," said Hector. He pointed to a poster on the wall.

Stop | Think | Write

VOCABULARY

What does Maria find peculiar about the caterpillars?

_____

_____

_____

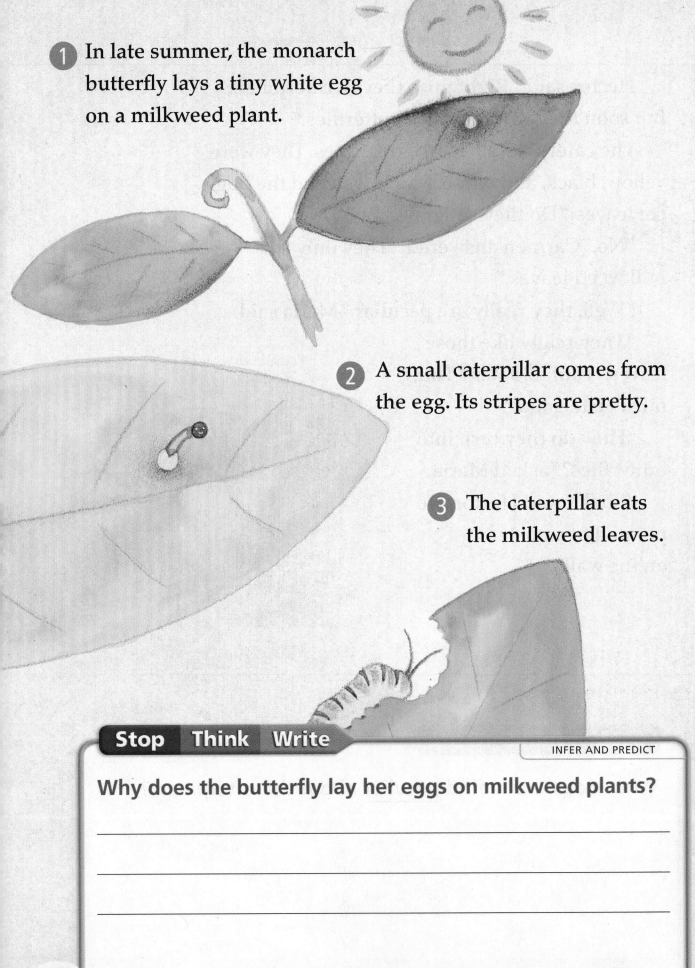

1 In late summer, the monarch butterfly lays a tiny white egg on a milkweed plant.

2 A small caterpillar comes from the egg. Its stripes are pretty.

3 The caterpillar eats the milkweed leaves.

Stop Think Write

INFER AND PREDICT

Why does the butterfly lay her eggs on milkweed plants?

_____

_____

_____

4 The caterpillar grows. Its old skin falls off. This looks icky!

5 The big caterpillar hangs itself upside down. It wraps itself in a green and gold case.

6 In about two weeks, the case breaks open. Out comes a monarch butterfly! It is really beautiful!

Stop | **Think** | **Write**

SEQUENCE OF EVENTS

What happens before the caterpillar's skin falls off?

_____

_____

_____

"I see now," Maria said. "The butterflies find those leaves **nourishing**. Will we keep the butterflies?"

"No," Mrs. Woods said. "They fly to Mexico for the winter. It's nice and warm there." Mrs. Woods went on. "We have a problem. They should have made the trip before. It is getting cold. Now they won't find enough food along the way."

"I'm afraid they will die," Pat said. "Could we mail them?"

"We can't put living things in the mail," Hector said.

Stop **Think** **Write**

STORY STRUCTURE

Why is the class worried about the butterflies?

_____

_____

_____

Maria had an idea. She said, "My father **intends** to go to Mexico soon. He flies an airplane. That's his job."

"Great!" said Mrs. Woods. "Will you talk to him about our problem?"

That night, Maria asked her dad for help. He said he could **assist** them. Once the caterpillars turned into butterflies, Maria's dad came to pick them up. They were in boxes with tiny holes.

"I'll be very careful with them," he said. "We leave in three hours. Tonight, I will set them free in Mexico."

Stop | Think | Write

VOCABULARY

Explain how Maria's father intends to help the butterflies.

_____

_____

_____

259

The next day, everyone was excited.

"Did the butterflies get there?" they all asked.

Maria smiled widely. "Yes! Everything went well. Dad opened the boxes, and away they flew."

"I can't believe they're in Mexico now!" said Sara.

"Yes! Maria, we are so happy that our little friends are home," said Mrs. Woods as she pointed to Mexico on the globe. "We are very happy that you are part of this class."

Maria smiled. She felt right at home.

Stop | **Think** | **Write**

How is the problem solved?

_____

_____

_____

Look Back and Respond

1 **What do Maria's words and actions tell you about her?**

_____

_____

_____

Hint

Clues you can use are on almost every page!

2 **What is the problem in the story?**

_____

_____

_____

Hint

For a clue, see page 258.

3 **How does Maria help solve the problem?**

_____

_____

_____

Hint

For a clue, see page 259.

4 **How does Maria feel after she has helped solve the problem?**

_____

_____

_____

Hint

For a clue, see page 260.

Be a Reading Detective!

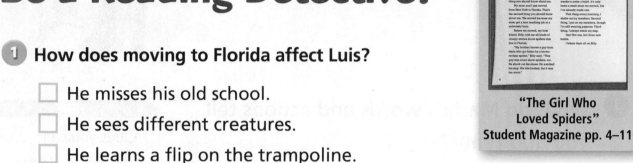

Return to

"The Girl Who Loved Spiders"
Student Magazine pp. 4–11

1 **How does moving to Florida affect Luis?**

☐ He misses his old school.

☐ He sees different creatures.

☐ He learns a flip on the trampoline.

Prove It! What evidence in the story supports your answer?
Check the boxes. ☑   Make notes.

Evidence	Notes
☐ what Luis says and thinks	
☐ what Billy has told him	
☐ what happens to Luis with Ashanti	

Write About It!

STORY STRUCTURE

Answer question 1 using evidence from the text.

_____

_____

_____

_____

_____

_____

_____

2 **What important lesson about life does the story teach?**

☐ You can learn a lot from your neighbors.

☐ Learning about something can change what you think.

☐ Most spiders are not dangerous.

Prove It! What evidence in the story supports your answer? Check the boxes. ☑ Make notes.

Evidence	Notes
☐ what Luis thinks about spiders at the beginning of the story	
☐ what he thinks about spiders at the end of the story	
☐	

Write About It!

THEME

Answer question 2 using evidence from the text.

_____

_____

_____

_____

_____

_____

_____

alert
opportunities
scarce
shortage
species

Ecosystems

All of the living things in an area are part of the area's ecosystem. The plants and animals depend on each other to survive.

Some **species** are found in more than one ecosystem. For example, many types of birds nest in one place and feed in another.

In rainforests, water is plentiful. In deserts, it is **scarce**. Different places support very different kinds of life. A **shortage** of food or other changes may cause problems for plants and animals. If we don't protect them, some plants and animals may be lost forever.

Scientists are **alert** to changes in an environment. They look for **opportunities** to protect the plants and animals there.

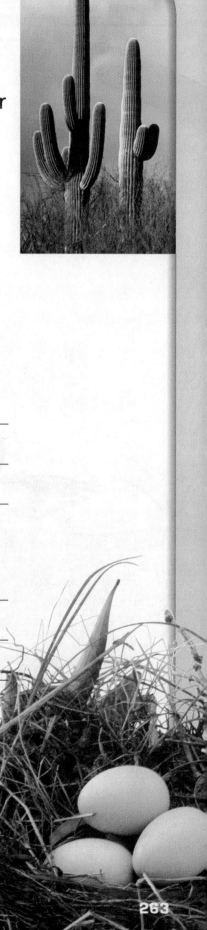

1 A _____ of food or another change to a place may cause some plants or animals to be lost forever.

2 Some _____ of birds nest in one area and feed in another area.

3 In the desert, water is _____.

4 What <u>opportunities</u> do you have to show off your talents?

_____

_____

_____

5 What can you do to stay <u>alert</u> in class?

_____

_____

_____

The Life of a Pond

by Lynn Frankel

A pond is full of life. Look in and around a pond. Millions of living things make their homes there. The pond and what lives in it make up an ecosystem. It is a community of plants and animals in one place.

Each of the animals is busy trying to stay alive. All seek food and shelter. They are always **alert** to dangers. They hide from animals that want to eat them, and they try to keep their young safe.

Stop   Think   Write

MAIN IDEAS AND DETAILS

What is an ecosystem?

_____

_____

_____

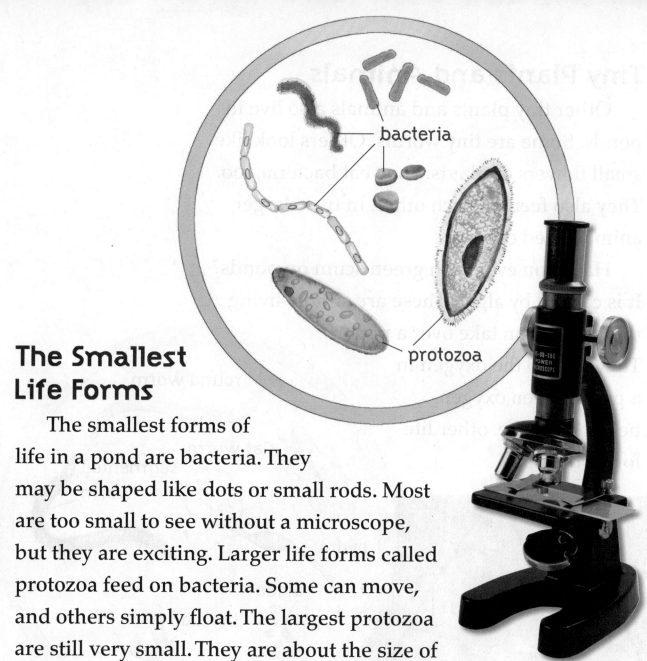

bacteria

protozoa

The Smallest Life Forms

The smallest forms of life in a pond are bacteria. They may be shaped like dots or small rods. Most are too small to see without a microscope, but they are exciting. Larger life forms called protozoa feed on bacteria. Some can move, and others simply float. The largest protozoa are still very small. They are about the size of two or three small letters in a newspaper!

Stop **Think** **Write**

MAIN IDEAS AND DETAILS

Which life forms eat bacteria?

_____

_____

_____

Tiny Plants and Animals

Other tiny plants and animals also live in ponds. Some are tiny worms. Others look like small flowers or plants. They eat bacteria, too. They also feed on each other. In turn, larger animals feed on them.

Have you ever seen green scum on ponds? It is caused by algae. These are simple living things that can take over a pond. They use up the oxygen in a pond. When oxygen becomes **scarce**, other life forms die out.

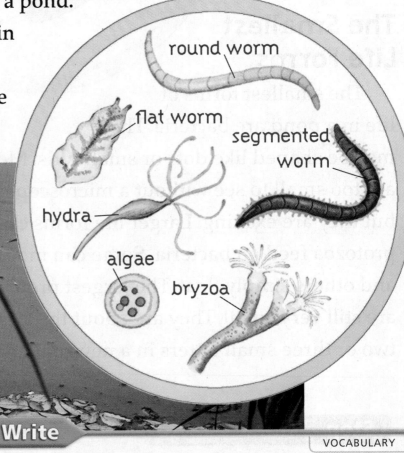

round worm

flat worm

segmented worm

hydra

algae

bryzoa

Stop **Think** **Write**

VOCABULARY

What might happen if food for animals becomes <u>scarce</u>?

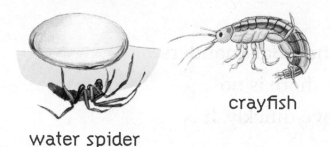

water spider

crayfish

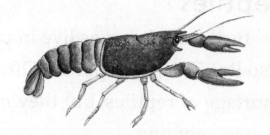

freshwater shrimp

Arthropods and Fish

Arthropods live in ponds, too. Spiders, shrimp, and insects belong in this group. They use legs or tails to move. They hold onto prey with their mouths and claws.

Many kinds of insects live in ponds. Some always live under the water. Others, such as dragonflies, live their lives in stages. When young, they are in the water. Then their bodies change, and they take to the air.

Fish eat insects in a pond. The size and number of fish depend on how big the pond is and what else lives there.

| Stop | Think | Write |

CAUSE AND EFFECT

Why might a small number of insects in a pond mean fewer fish?

_____

_____

_____

Reptiles

Turtles and snakes live in ponds. Salamanders also live in or near ponds. Often there is no **shortage** of reptiles, but they move quickly. It is rare to spot one.

Reptiles that live in ponds are not in the water all the time. They lay their eggs on land. Animals living near the pond have **opportunities** to feed on young reptiles and reptile eggs.

Stop **Think** **Write**

CONCLUSIONS

What might be a rare sight in your neighborhood?

_____

_____

_____

_____

Frogs

Frogs are interesting animals. They lay their eggs in the water. The eggs become tadpoles. A tadpole hatches with gills like a fish. Then the gills close, and the tadpole begins to breathe air. It grows leg buds and loses its tail. After a few weeks, it becomes a frog.

Adult frogs eat small fish and even mice. Snakes, turtles, raccoons, and birds hunt frogs.

Stop	Think	Write

SEQUENCE OF EVENTS

What happens to tadpoles just before they become frogs?

_____

_____

_____

Cycles

Animals depend on each other to survive. Big animals eat small ones. Small animals eat still smaller ones. This cycle is called a food chain.

Ponds have a life cycle, too. Over time, rain washes things into the pond. It slowly fills up. As time goes by, a pond may turn into a marsh. One day it might disappear altogether.

A lack of life in a pond may be a sign of trouble. Maybe weeds have taken over. Maybe one **species** has wiped out all the others. Some people work hard to keep ponds healthy. They know that the pond is an important little world.

Stop | **Think** | **Write**

MAIN IDEAS AND DETAILS

What is the main idea of this section?

_____

_____

_____

Look Back and Respond

1 How can algae take over a pond?

_____

_____

_____

Hint

For a clue, see page 266.

2 Write two details that explain how a food chain works.

_____

_____

_____

Hint

For a clue, see page 270.

3 Name two animals that live in ponds. On what does each animal feed?

_____

_____

_____

Hint

Clues are on almost every page!

4 What is this selection mainly about?

_____

_____

_____

Hint

Reread the title. Think about what most details in the text are about.

Be a Reading Detective!

Return to

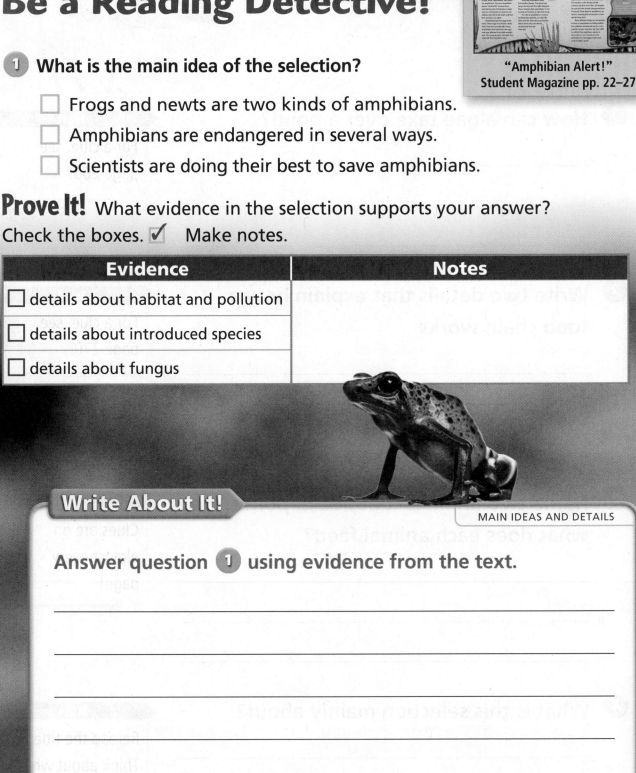

"Amphibian Alert!"
Student Magazine pp. 22–27

1 **What is the main idea of the selection?**

☐ Frogs and newts are two kinds of amphibians.

☐ Amphibians are endangered in several ways.

☐ Scientists are doing their best to save amphibians.

Prove It! What evidence in the selection supports your answer?
Check the boxes. ✓ Make notes.

Evidence	Notes
☐ details about habitat and pollution	
☐ details about introduced species	
☐ details about fungus	

Write About It!

MAIN IDEAS AND DETAILS

Answer question **1** using evidence from the text.

_____

_____

_____

_____

_____

_____

② **Why did the author write the selection?**

☐ to encourage people to raise amphibians

☐ to describe many kinds of amphibians

☐ to encourage people to help amphibians

Prove It! What evidence in the selection supports your answer?
Check the boxes. ☑ Make notes.

Evidence	Notes
☐ details about amphibians	
☐ threats to amphibians	
☐ ways people can help amphibians	

Write About It!

AUTHOR'S PURPOSE

Answer question ② using evidence from the text.

_____

_____

_____

_____

_____

_____

apologize
display
genuine
obstacles
vast

Museums

The largest natural history museum in the world is in Washington, D.C. It was started in 1910. The museum has more than 125 million items. It has not always had that many. The museum has been able to expand. Now it has a **vast** collection. People give items and money.

The museum's collection is displayed in six separate halls. One hall is for gems and minerals. In that hall, the Hope Diamond is on **display**. Another hall is for mammals. It is full of **genuine** skeletons. Each exhibit is in a glass case. That way, nobody has to **apologize** for breaking anything.

Keeping everything in good condition is one of the **obstacles** the museum has to face. Bones must be dusted. Gems must be polished. Making sure 125 million items look good is a big job. It takes hundreds of workers and scientists.

1 When items are in glass cases, no one

has to _____ for breaking
anything.

2 People have helped the museum build a

_____ collection.

3 The Hope Diamond is on

_____ in the hall
for gems and minerals.

4 What <u>obstacles</u> might you face on your way
to school?

_____

_____

_____

5 Explain the difference between a <u>genuine</u>
dinosaur skeleton and a dinosaur model.

_____

_____

_____

In the Museum

by Lynn Frankel

Carlos and Kim are visiting the museum with their teacher, Mr. Diego. The museum has a new dinosaur exhibit.

During their visit, Carlos and Kim are going to talk to people who work at the museum. They'll learn a lot of facts about the exhibit. They are going to report what they have learned to their class.

Stop **Think** **Write**

STORY STRUCTURE

What kind of exhibit will Carlos and Kim learn about during their museum visit?

_____

_____

_____

The students meet Mrs. Reed in the lobby. She is the director of the museum. She introduces her assistant, Mr. Fox.

Mr. Diego thinks his students might be nervous. He asks the first question. "Why did you decide to have a dinosaur exhibit?"

Mrs. Reed smiles. "Well, dinosaurs are amazing! They became extinct long ago, but people are still fascinated by them."

Stop Think Write

FACT AND OPINION

What opinion does the director give about dinosaurs?

_____

_____

_____

Kim reads the first question on her notepad. "Did you face any **obstacles** getting the exhibit ready?"

Mr. Fox nods. "Our biggest one was finding all the objects we wanted to show."

"Where did you get them?" Carlos asks.

"Mostly from other museums," Mr. Fox explains. "I spent months writing e-mails and letters to museums around the world."

Mr. Fox leads the group to the main **display**. It shows some **genuine** dinosaur skeletons. It also has life-sized dinosaur models.

Stop **Think** **Write**

STORY STRUCTURE

Where did the museum get most of the objects in the dinosaur exhibit?

_____

_____

_____

276

"We spent a lot of time thinking about the contents of this display," Mr. Fox says. "At first we just had the skeletons. Then we decided we wanted to show something more."

"We wanted to show what the world was like when dinosaurs were alive. We decided to expand the exhibit. We added models of other dinosaurs. We also added plants to show more of the dinosaurs' **vast** habitat," says Mrs. Reed.

"It looks great," says Kim. "Everyone here seems to think so."

Stop | Think | Write

CITE TEXT EVIDENCE

How did Mrs. Reed and Mr. Fox expand the main exhibit?

_____

_____

_____

Mrs. Reed leads them into the next room. This one has dinosaurs, too.

"Here are two of our guides," says Mrs. Reed. "They show people around the museum and tell them about each exhibit. I'm going to leave you in their care."

"Will they know as much as you and Mr. Fox?" asks Kim.

Mrs. Reed laughs. "We train all of our guides. They know our dinosaurs inside out! Don't worry. They'll be able to answer any questions you have."

Stop **Think** **Write**

MAIN IDEA AND DETAILS

What do the museum guides do?

_____

_____

_____

Carlos asks about the row of screens in the room. "This part of the exhibit is interactive," the guide replies. "There are games that teach you about dinosaurs. They get everyone really involved."

"Here's a dinosaur that flew," the guide continues. "We're showing a movie about it. I have to **apologize**, though. The next movie doesn't start for another two hours."

"We can't stay that long," says Kim. "I wish we could."

"That's okay. We'll be coming back next week with the whole class," says Mr. Diego.

Stop　Think　Write

VOCABULARY

Why does the guide apologize?

_____

_____

_____

Mr. Diego and his students go to say goodbye to Mrs. Reed. "We have to get back to school now," says Mr. Diego. "Thanks so much for your help."

"Yes, thank you," Carlos adds. "We have plenty to report back to our class."

Kim shakes Mrs. Reed's hand. "Your exhibit is awesome! I can't wait to come next week!"

Everyone waves goodbye. Everyone, that is, except the dinosaurs.

Stop **Think** **Write**

STORY STRUCTURE

What are Kim and Carlos going to do when they get back to school?

_____

_____

_____

Look Back and Respond

1 Why might people want to visit the new dinosaur exhibit at the museum?

Hint
Clues you can use are on almost every page!

_____

_____

_____

2 Name one obstacle that Mrs. Reed and Mr. Fox faced as they got the exhibit ready.

Hint
For clues, see pages 276 and 277.

_____

_____

_____

3 Write a fact from the story.

Hint
A fact is a statement that can be proved.

_____

_____

_____

4 Write an opinion from the story.

Hint
An opinion is a statement that cannot be proved.

_____

_____

_____

Be a Reading Detective!

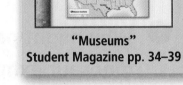

Return to

"Museums"
Student Magazine pp. 34–39

1 **Which facts support the author's opinion that museums are wonderful?** Choose every correct answer.

- ☐ They present interesting facts.
- ☐ They show exciting exhibits.
- ☐ They provide new experiences.

Prove It! What evidence in the selection supports your answer?
Check the boxes. ✓ Make notes.

Evidence	Notes
☐ what you can do at each museum	
☐ what you can see at each museum	

Write About It!

FACT AND OPINION

Answer question **1** using evidence from the text.

_____

_____

_____

_____

_____

_____

_____

2 **What is the main idea about the Field Museum on page 37?**

☐ Sue is one of the museum's most interesting exhibits.

☐ People can get close to Sue's skull.

☐ The museum has more than twenty million interesting items.

Prove It! What evidence in the selection supports your answer?
Check the boxes. ☑ Make notes.

Evidence	Notes
☐ details about Sue's skeleton	
☐ details about Sue's skull	
☐ details about other exhibits	

Write About It!

MAIN IDEAS AND DETAILS

Answer question 2 using evidence from the text.

_____

_____

_____

_____

_____

_____

In the Mojave Desert

Desert weather is extreme. The summer sun's ❶ _____ light can make temperatures reach 130 degrees. Winter temperatures may drop to freezing.

Hikers in the desert often wear long sleeves. It may seem like a bad idea, but it is not. The fabric can protect their skin. It can also keep them from losing too much water from their bodies.

Desert animals are used to the heat and cold. They rest in the shade by day and hunt the **2** _____ for food at night. People may not be **3** _____ with leaving home only at night. Desert animals, though, have to do it to survive.

Joshua trees grow only in America's Mojave Desert. So if you see one, you can have **4** _____ that you are in the Mojave!

The old silver mines in the Mojave closed down years ago. Everyone soon left the towns. Today, we call these empty towns ghost towns. They have become a **5** _____ of the old West.

A Stop in the Desert

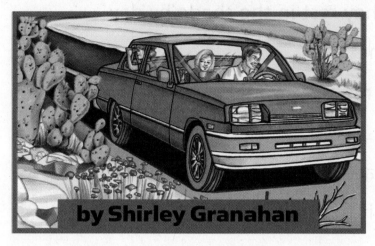

by Shirley Granahan

"We're in the Mojave Desert now," Dad said. "Jodi, keep your camera ready for great shots!"

We were on our way to visit my cousins in California. Dad had chosen to drive through the desert, which was unfamiliar **territory** to us.

I had seen pictures of the Mojave's **symbol**, the Joshua tree, in a guide book. Now, I could take my own! I snapped shots of the tree through the car window. "I love the desert," I said.

"We knew you'd like it," said Mom. "That's why we decided to go this way."

Stop | Think | Write

STORY STRUCTURE

Why is the family driving through the desert?

_____

_____

_____

All of a sudden, the car made a funny noise. It rolled to a stop. "Oh, no!" Dad said. "Don't worry. I'll check it out."

He slowly lifted the car hood. There was a cloud of steam! "You two go take pictures," he said. "I should have this up and running in no time."

I took a picture of a cactus. The **brilliant** desert sun beat down on me. "It's really hot, Mom!" I said. "How do these plants survive?"

Stop   Think   Write

VOCABULARY

How does the brilliant desert sun make Jodi feel?

_____

_____

_____

"They adapt," said Mom. "A desert doesn't get much rain. So, a cactus soaks up water when it does rain. The cactus's thick, waxy outside holds the water in. Then the plant can use it later."

"I hope Dad knows as much about cars as you do about plants," I laughed.

"Let's see how he's doing," Mom said.

We walked back to the car. Dad seemed to have lost his **confidence**. "I can't get the car to start," he said. "We'd better call for help."

Stop **Think** **Write**

CITE TEXT EVIDENCE

How does the waxy outside of a cactus help the plant?

_____

_____

_____

Mom tried her cell phone. There was no signal. "What do we do now?" I asked.

"We just hope that someone comes along," Mom replied.

"What if no one comes?" I asked. "We're pretty far off the main road."

Dad smiled, "Don't worry, Jodi. We'll be fine."

"I'm so thirsty," I said.

Mom got out a bottle of water, and we all had a drink. Still the sun beat down, hotter and hotter. "I have an idea," Dad said.

Stop Think Write

UNDERSTANDING CHARACTERS

How does Jodi feel about being stuck in the desert? Explain.

_____

_____

_____

_____

Dad took blankets from the trunk. He hung one between two cactus plants. "This will give us some shade," he said, **satisfied** with his work. He put the other blanket on the ground. We sat down.

Hours went by, but no cars came. "Can we eat our sandwiches now?" I asked.

"Eating will only make you thirstier," Mom said. "It's better to just sit in the shade and stay still."

Stop   Think   Write

VOCABULARY

Why is Dad <u>satisfied</u> with his work?

_____

_____

_____

Soon the sun vanished behind a hill. The night air was colder. "I was hot before and now I'm cold!" I said. "Is it always like this?"

"Yes," Dad said. "Deserts are hot by day and cold by night. We should get back in the car."

Dad grabbed the blankets and we got into the car. I curled up on the back seat. Just then, I heard a howl. "What's that?" I asked.

"Just a coyote," Dad said. "Most desert animals come out at night when it's cooler."

Stop **Think** **Write**

CONCLUSIONS AND GENERALIZATIONS

Why do most desert animals come out at night?

_____

_____

_____

I guess I fell asleep. The next thing I remember, a police officer knocked on our car window. "Are you okay?" he asked.

Dad explained what had happened. The officer called for help. As we waited, I snapped shots of jackrabbits, lizards, and kangaroo rats in the early morning light. I knew they would disappear into shady spots when the sun got too hot.

I was almost sad we would soon be leaving the desert. I'd learned how to adapt to desert life just like the plants and animals that live there!

Stop Think Write

UNDERSTANDING CHARACTERS

Does Jodi enjoy her night in the desert? Explain.

_____

_____

_____

Look Back and Respond

1 How does Jodi feel when she first sees the Mojave Desert?

Hint

For a clue, see page 284.

_____

_____

_____

2 How is a cactus adapted to survive with very little rain?

Hint

For clues, see pages 285 and 286.

_____

_____

_____

3 How would you describe Jodi's mother?

Hint

For clues, see pages 284, 286, and 288.

_____

_____

_____

4 What does Jodi learn in the story?

Hint

For a clue, see page 290.

_____

_____

_____

Be a Reading Detective!

Return to

"Save Timber Woods!"
Student Magazine pp. 48–55

1 **Which adjective best describes Gina at the start of the play?**

☐ selfish   ☐ sensible
☐ enthusiastic   ☐ friendly

Prove It! What evidence in the play supports your answer?
Check the boxes. ✓   Make notes.

Evidence	Notes
☐ what Gina says at first	
☐ what Gina does at first	
☐ how others react to Gina	

Write About It!

UNDERSTANDING CHARACTERS

Answer question 1 using evidence from the text.

_____

_____

_____

_____

_____

_____

2 **Which two effects would cutting down Timber Woods have?**

☐ The animals that live there would have no home.

☐ The risk of flooding would increase.

☐ The town would make a lot of money.

Prove It! What evidence in the play supports your answer?
Check the boxes. ☑   Make notes.

Evidence	Notes
☐ what the friends read	
☐ what the friends already know	

Write About It!

CAUSE AND EFFECT

Answer question **2** **using evidence from the text.**

_____

_____

_____

_____

_____

_____

_____

291B

✓ **TARGET VOCABULARY**

effort
informed
progress
resources
shallow

Hiking in the Wilderness

Hiking in the wilderness is worth the **1** _____ . You'll be rewarded for your hard work. Make sure you have maps and supplies. It is best to be **2** _____ about the kind of land you will be crossing.

If an area is hilly and rocky, wear sturdy boots. You'll be less likely to twist an ankle if you have the right footgear. The best way to make **3** _____ up a mountain is to take breaks. That way, you will not get too tired.

When you hike, you might come across a stream. It is safe to cross if the water is **4** _____ . If not, you will have to find a bridge to help you get to the other side.

No matter where you go, make sure to take plenty of water. In some places, the natural **5** _____ do not include water. Hikers should drink a lot of liquids.

A Boat in the Wilderness

by K. T. Archer

I was excited. My mom, my brother, and I were going on a trip to the Everglades. We would even be sleeping on a houseboat!

The Everglades is a large swamp. A swamp is an area of land that always has **shallow** water covering it. I looked at a book about the area. The swamp has natural **resources**, like fuel and minerals.

"The best way to explore a swamp is on a houseboat," Mom told us. "You'll love it."

Pedro was worried. "I get seasick."

"A swamp isn't rough," Mom promised.

Stop | Think | Write

VOCABULARY

Do you think the family will see whales swimming in the **shallow** swamp water? Explain.

_____

_____

_____

294

When we got to the Everglades, the owner of the boat was waiting. His name was Joe.

"Welcome, Gomez family!" he called out. "This will be your home for four days."

I stared at the water. It looked like blue glass.

Joe said, "Come aboard! I'll show you around. This is the stern, the back of the boat. That's the bow, the front."

"Where are the sails?" I asked.

Joe laughed. "This boat doesn't have sails. It has a gas engine. Still, it takes a lot of **effort** to operate the boat."

Stop   Think   Write

INFER AND PREDICT

What kinds of jobs might you have to do on a boat like Joe's?

_____

_____

_____

I looked around the cabin. It was like a little house on top of the boat. There were chairs, a table, and special beds called bunks. The lower deck was outside. It went all around the boat. The upper deck was on the cabin's roof. You could see for miles from there.

Joe explained how everything worked. He showed us how to steer the boat. He also showed us how to keep the boat from floating away. You do that by dropping the anchor.

Stop | Think | Write

CONCLUSIONS AND GENERALIZATIONS

What do you think happens when the anchor is dropped into the water?

_____

_____

_____

I asked, "Are there many animals in the swamp?"

"Sure there are," said Joe.

"Are there alligators?" I continued.

"Lots of them!" laughed Joe. Pedro looked horrified. "Oh, I forgot you don't know so much about the swamp. Don't worry. Anyone who is **informed** knows that alligators can't get on a boat like this."

Pretty soon, we were ready. Joe stepped back on land, and we were on our own. Mom was the captain. She steered the boat away from the dock.

Stop | Think | Write

CONCLUSIONS AND GENERALIZATIONS

Why do you think the narrator's mother is the captain?

_____

_____

_____

We passed through open water. We went through narrow strips. Grassy land was all around us. Birds were everywhere. They hopped in and out of the water, looking for fish. Sure enough, there were alligators, too! They didn't bother us, but their long teeth looked scary.

Everyone took turns cooking. We made simple meals, like soup and grilled cheese. Mom told me I was making **progress** in the kitchen.

Stop **Think** **Write**

VOCABULARY

What does Mom mean when she says the narrator is making **progress** in the kitchen?

_____

_____

_____

I loved eating and sleeping on the boat. I didn't like the bugs, though! We stayed inside in the early morning and early evening. That's when the bugs came around. They made a thick cloud. It was the only part of the trip we didn't like. That was a small price to pay for so much fun.

Stop | **Think** | **Write**

CLARIFY

What does the narrator mean when he says the bugs make "a thick cloud"?

_____

_____

_____

After four days, we were back where we had started. Joe came to meet us at the dock.

"How did it go?" he asked us.

"The Everglades are beautiful," I answered.

"I love boats!" said Pedro. "Can we come back next year, Mom?"

"We'll see," said Mom. "Thanks, Joe. We all had a great time."

Stop Think Write

Why do you think Pedro wants to go back to the Everglades next summer?

_____

_____

_____

Look Back and Respond

1 How would you describe the narrator?

_____

_____

_____

Hint

Clues you can use are on almost every page!

2 Why doesn't the Gomez family have to worry about alligators?

_____

_____

_____

Hint

For a clue, see page 297.

3 Why does the family stay inside the boat in the morning and evening?

_____

_____

_____

Hint

For a clue, see page 299.

4 What advantages does a houseboat have over a normal boat?

_____

_____

_____

Hint

For clues, see pages 296, 298, and 299.

Be a Reading Detective!

Return to

"Mystery at Reed's Pond"
Student Magazine pp. 64–71

1 How many turtles did the boy on the bike leave at the pond?

☐ one ☐ three

☐ two ☐ no way to know

Prove It! What evidence in the story supports your answer?
Check the boxes. ✓ Make notes.

Evidence	Notes
☐ what the pond patrol saw happen	
☐ how many turtles were caught	
☐ what the students did not see happen	

Write About It!

CONCLUSIONS AND GENERALIZATIONS

Answer question **1** using evidence from the text.

_____

_____

_____

_____

_____

_____

_____

301A

2 **What does the author want readers to understand?**

☐ Animals that don't belong can harm the environment.

☐ Solving a mystery can result in a reward.

☐ People grow tired of pets that get too big.

Prove It! What evidence in the story supports your answer?
Check the boxes. ✓ Make notes.

Evidence	Notes
☐ where the red-eared slider's natural habitat is	
☐ where Reed's Pond is	
☐ what Mr. Roberts tells the students	

Write About It!

AUTHOR'S PURPOSE

Answer question 2 using evidence from the text.

_____

_____

_____

_____

_____

_____

_____

Summarize Strategy

When you **summarize**, briefly retell the important ideas in a text.

- Use your own words.

- Organize ideas in a way that makes sense.

- Do not change the meaning of the text.

- Make your summary short. Use only a few sentences.

Analyze/Evaluate Strategy

You can **analyze** and **evaluate** a text. Study the text carefully. Then form an opinion about it.

1. Analyze the text. Look at the ideas. Think about what the author tells you.

   - What are the important facts and details?

   - How are the ideas organized?

   - What does the author want you to know?

2. Evaluate the text. Decide what is important. Then form an opinion.

   - How do you feel about what you read?

   - Do you agree with the author's ideas?

   - Did the author succeed in reaching his or her goals?

Infer/Predict Strategy

You can make an **inference**. Figure out what the author does not tell you.

• Think about the clues in the text.

• Think about what you already know.

You can make a **prediction**. Use text clues to figure out what will happen next.

Monitor/Clarify Strategy

You can **monitor** what you read. Pay attention to how well you understand the text.

If you read a part that doesn't make sense, find a way to **clarify** it. Clear up what you don't understand.

• Use what you already know.

• Reread or read ahead. Find clues in the text.

• Read more slowly.

• Ask questions about the text.

Question Strategy

Ask yourself **questions** before, during, and after you read. Look for answers.

Some questions to ask:

- What does the author mean here?

- Who or what is this about?

- Why did this happen?

- What is the main idea?

- How does this work?

Visualize Strategy

You can **visualize** as you read. Use text details to make pictures in your mind.

- Use the author's words and your own knowledge to help.

- Make mental pictures of people, places, things, actions, and ideas.

PHOTO CREDITS